OPEN THE DOOR

Joyce Rupp

OPEN THE DOOR

A JOURNEY TO THE TRUE SELF

SORIN BOOKS  Notre Dame, Indiana

Scripture quotations are from the *New Revised Standard Version* of the Bible, copyright © 1993 and 1989 by the Division of Christian Education of the National Council of Churches of Christ in the U. S. A. Used by permission. All rights reserved.

Excerpts in Weeks Three and Five from *Show Yourself to My Soul* by Rabindranath Tagore, translated by James Talarovic, copyright © 2002 are reprinted with permission of Sorin Books, Notre Dame, IN.

"Look at Me" by Mary Katherine Lidle is used with permission of Kathleen Dolan. All rights reserved.

Acknowledgments are continued on page 213.

www.sorinbooks.com

ISBN-10 1-933495-14-6 ISBN-13 978-1-933495-14-9

Cover and text design by Brian C. Conley.

Printed and bound in the United States of America.

Library of Congress Cataloging-in-Publication Data
Rupp, Joyce.
  Open the door : a journey to the true self / Joyce Rupp.
     p. cm.
  Includes bibliographical references.
  ISBN-13: 978-1-933495-14-9 (pbk.)
  ISBN-10: 1-933495-14-6 (pbk.)
  1. Spiritual life. I. Title.
  BL624.R85 2008
  248.4--dc22

                    2008012932

To

THERESA
BELOVED COUSIN

JENNIFER
WISE SPIRITUAL GUIDE

DOROTHY
MENTOR OF GENEROSITY

EACH ONE
OPENED THE DOOR
OF MY HEART

ACKNOWLEDGMENTS

Open the Door had a lengthy gestation. Eight years ago *U.S. Catholic* graciously published an article of mine on the theme of opening doors to spiritual growth. Since that time, I have given numerous retreats and conferences in which I've invited participants to reflect on the symbol of doors in relation to their inner journey. The participants' creative ideas and enriching comments seeded the contents of this book.

At the same time, visitors to my website also contributed valuable insights and information that I gathered and added to my writing. I'm particularly indebted to Audrey Brown, Vicki Limberg-Buerkett, Judith Campbell, Suzanne Delaney, Don and Evelyn DeLutis, Kathleen Dolan, Meg Draeger, Annette Drzala, Ruth Foster, Linda Hale, Shelley Den Haan, Mary Mahoney, Jenny Malatesta, Dorothy Romines, Denise Kollias, Marti Page, Beth Patterson, Dan Pearson, Austin Repath, Carol Reuter, Nancy Singh, Abbey Swalwell, Katy Swalwell, Ann Steadman, Concepta A. Tobin, Joanne White, Sr. Bernadette Marie Zandonatti, Pam Zaremba, and all who wrote and offered their stories related to "doors."

Besides these beneficial resources, I gained valuable help in the final drafting from a group of eight individuals whom I invited to experience the process of praying with *Open the Door*. Mary Ferring, Mary Jones, Mark Lindahl, Kathy Reardon, Kristy Smith, Mary Routh, Rodger Routh, and Paul Witmer were just what I needed. During the six weeks in which we met, they gifted me with their professional expertise and spiritual experience, helping me to refine and improve the text.

Valuable input and support came from Roy Boucher, Wayne Gubbels, Jon Hrabe, David Manders, Nancy Marsh, and Macrina Wiederkehr. My time in sacred places of beauty also aided the book's development: many thanks to Aileen Martin and the Sisters of Mercy in New Zealand, the praying community at Shantivanum in Easton, Kansas, and the staff at Mercy Center in Madison, Connecticut. My community (the Servants of Mary), the beloved women of Morning Midwives, my friends and relatives (especially my sister, Lois Schallau), my website manager Faye Williamsen, and Janet Barnes (the most faithful pray-er I know) have continually cheered me on in the writing of this book.

The staff at Ave Maria Press/Sorin Books contributed immensely to making this book possible. Publisher Tom Grady encouraged me from its beginning. Editor Robert Hamma expertly guided me through the final preparations. Mary Andrews and Julie Cinninger continually amazed me with their creative marketing skills.

As I bring this book forth, I am keenly aware that its pages bear the influence of countless persons whose names are not mentioned. If you have entered the door of my life, the touch of your presence is here. Thank you, one and all.

Contents

INTRODUCTION

Open the door of your treasure today,
for tomorrow the key will not be in your hands.
—Sa'di

DO YOU REMEMBER the last time you opened a door? Probably not. Doors are a natural part of daily life. We rarely notice the movement of passing through the space they allow for our comings and goings. There are exceptions, of course, when our arms are full of groceries or we've forgotten our keys, but normally we breeze through these helpful openings oblivious to what we're doing. Yet, doors are an integral part of life. If we are mobile and active, never a day goes by without moving through numerous doorways. Think of the physical doors that are a part of your day, particularly the ones since you awoke this morning. Undoubtedly there are many.

How essential and beneficial doors are. They open and close, provide accommodating passageways to where we want to go, offer protection from unwanted elements, and ensure a certain amount of safety and privacy. Doors are even useful for helping define where we are physically: indoors, outdoors, next door, at the front door or back door. There is a potential power to doors. We can use them as barriers of control with the ability to shut out, or allow them to be welcoming hosts with the freedom to come and go.

By simply looking at a door, it can connect us to the events that mapped our developing lives. My friend Mary bought an old barn gate from the farm of her childhood to place in her urban garden. "The gate

1

summons nostalgia for the farm," Mary tells me. The odors of the cattle yard, along with the animals and farm activities, quickly return to her when she looks at the gate. Similarly, in an article sent to me by Sr. Concepta Tobin, Helen O'Connell writes about a half-century-old door she arranged to have sent from Ireland to England. This traveling door now resides in her current home with the original key still in the lock. Why did O'Connell do this? The door carries her childhood memories. "Just to touch it, I can see the little girl who felt so big when she could reach the knocker," writes O'Connell. "I can see my mother, going to turn the key when a neighbor would call to her and still with her hand on the key she could talk for ages. I can see myself running out that door to my First Communion, my first job, a date, my wedding and my heart doing a summersault when I'd return home from England and see the door."

Doors give us an opportunity to make connections and find meaning in life. No wonder this image slips easily into our metaphorical language, providing ways to describe changes of attitude and activity. We "get a foot in the door," find "the door of opportunity," wonder what's happening "behind closed doors," and speak of "coming in the back door." Only yesterday I heard someone remark, "When I closed the door on my last job, a whole new world opened up for me."

How I Discovered the Image of the Door

The image of a door first intrigued me when I was praying the "O Antiphons" during the season of Advent. This mosaic of hope-filled verses, one for each of the seven days prior to Christmas, refers symbolically to Christ's incarnation. The antiphon for December 20 awakened me to the door's symbolism:

> *O Key of David* and Scepter of the House of Israel
> who opens and no one shuts, who shuts and no one opens:
> Come break down the prison walls of death
> for those who dwell in darkness and
> the shadow of death; deliver your captive people into freedom.

As I prayed this antiphon, certain words leapt out: key, open, shut, walls of death, dwell in darkness, deliver into freedom. These words bid me deeper, to look again at who I thought I was and how I lived my life. They summoned me to ponder my inner prison, the places of unfreedom, the walls of resistance, and the doors of my heart that pleaded for a key to open them. The antiphon also reminded me of Christ, a central key to the door of my becoming spiritually free.

The image of the key opening a door to freedom led me to view the door as a potent symbol for spiritual growth. I was filled with questions: What needed to be unlocked in me? How could I increasingly release the strongholds of my mind and heart to discover more of my potential to be my best self? What doors had I opened in the past? Which ones had I shut? What closed doors were helpful, which ones held me back? On and on the questions went as I compared the movement of opening a door to my desire of being my authentic self in more complete union with the Holy One.

The questions that arose allowed me to see each opening to my deeper self as an occasion to learn and accept what is truest about who I am. There is great freedom in this process. It enables me to recognize my genuine self, the one God created me to be. This, in turn, leads to self-acceptance and inner harmony. At the same time, this freedom intensifies my longing to incorporate and live the wisdom teachings of Christ so my life can resonate with generous love.

Eventually this awareness of the door as a metaphor moved me to shape a retreat around it. To my surprise, this image kept expanding, taking on a life of its own. There seemed to be no end to the insights "a door" could reveal about spiritual growth. Such is the layered texture of imagery. Esther de Waal refers to its boundless capacity for finding meaning:

> The longer we stay with an image and dialogue with it, the more it will yield up. "A symbol should go on deepening," as Flannery O'Connor says. We have to wait for the image to find us. Sometimes it may come unbidden but more often we must expect to stay with it, and to be ready to go deeper, layer upon layer upon layer, always waiting expectantly.

This "layering" became apparent to me as the themes of this book evolved. Each week took me a little further and deeper in search of the authentic self.

Our Own Sacred Door

The Sufi poet Jalaluddin Rumi describes our soul-space as a magnificent cathedral where we are "sweet beyond telling." Saint Teresa of Avila views it as a castle. She notes, "I can find nothing with which to compare the great beauty of a soul . . . we can hardly form any conception of the soul's great dignity and beauty." Another way to speak about this inner sphere where our truest self and God dwell is with the words of scripture. In his letter to the Corinthians, Paul asks, "Do you not know that you are God's temple and that God's Spirit dwells in you?" (1 Cor 3:16).

The body is often referred to as a temple of God but our soul is also a wondrous residence. This hidden part of us, in union with divinity, is where our abundant goodness (our God-ness) exists. Jesuit paleontologist, Teilhard de Chardin, understood the necessity of opening the door inward to find and claim this goodness. Reflecting on his spiritual growth, Chardin observed this truth: "The deeper I descend into myself, the more I find God at the heart of my being." Thomas Merton worded it differently but noted the same thing: "To find love I must enter into the sanctuary where it is hidden, which is the mystery of God."

Cathedrals. Castles. Temples. However we describe our inner terrain, one thing is certain: we tend to live in just a few rooms of our inner landscape. The full person God created us to be contains more than we can imagine, but most of us dwell within only a small portion of the superb castle of ourselves. Opening the door of our heart allows us entrance to the vast treasure of who we are and to the divine presence within us. We have an immeasurable amount of love and tenderness in us if only we open the door to discover it. The same is true with the multitude of our other qualities and virtues. Each door we open helps us grow into the fullness of who we are. Each discovery moves us to contribute love in our world.

Our authentic self, which is in union with God, may seem out of reach. It never is. "Deep in ourselves is the true Self," writes Beatrice Bruteau, "and that true Self is not separate from, or even different from, the Source of Being." Always our truest self cries out to be known, loved, embraced, welcomed without judgment, and integrated into the way we live. When we open the door and go inside, God is there in the temple of our soul, in the ashram of our heart, in the cathedral of our being. Which is not to dismiss the reality of this same loving presence being fully alive in our external world. The Holy One is with us in *all* of life. Our purpose for opening the door inward is to help us know and claim who we are so we can more completely join with God in expressing this love in every part of our external world.

In Warner Sallman's artistic portrayal of Revelation 3:20, Jesus stands at a door and knocks, awaiting an invitation to enter. The door symbolizes the human heart or the deeper self, to which Jesus comes. In his painting, Sallman knowingly omitted the doorknob on the outside, indicating his belief that the door to the heart is only opened from within. According to the artist's portrayal, we hold the power of welcome or refusal. It is our choice.

While this ability of having a choice in opening the door is accurate, it is equally valid to note that sometimes uninvited and unwanted life circumstances push the door open to our inner self and propel us inside. This movement happens in those situations when we find ourselves unwillingly drawn to growth, pulled inward when we least expect by undesired experiences like a serious car accident, severe illness, betrayal in a committed relationship, or the death of a dear one. Whether we open the door freely or are shoved through it, opportunities arise for us to take God's hand and visit our inner territory. We learn and grow from every situation if we are open to it.

For Rabindranath Tagore the melody of his life directed him toward the divine. In one of his poems in the *Gitanjali,* he wrote:

> Ever in my life have I sought thee with my songs. It was they
> who led me from door to door, and with them I have felt about
> me, searching and touching my world.
> It was my songs that taught me all the lessons I ever learnt;

they showed me secret paths, they brought before my sight
many a star on the horizon of my heart.

Like Tagore with his songs, each part of life provides a door to our heart, revealing the path to spiritual growth. Countless doors open for us through myriad possibilities such as a profession of love, a meaningful prayer, a startling thought, a comforting emotion, a challenging dream, a pressing intuition, a peace-filled stillness, a provocative book, a glimpse of nature's beauty, or the voice of someone we encounter. These sources and others are doors leading to keener perception of ourselves and the One who dwells within. The Holy One is forever startling us with the prospect of further growth. Every moment invites us to discovery.

While we are urged repeatedly to swing open the doors to growth, it takes both intention and awareness to do so. We develop and hone this alertness through brief or extended pauses of silence, focused prayer, meaningful worship, deliberate reflection, and trust-filled dialogue with spiritual companions. Anytime we slow down, decrease our hurrying, or deliberately choose to stop and consider what is happening (or not happening) in our life, we are preparing ourselves to open the door of our heart. The divine visitor is waiting at the door. We need only to open it wide with our welcome.

WHAT IS THE HEART?

Heart implies emotion. Think of those hearts embossed on valentines. Yet, heart in the scriptural tradition connotes our entire internal, non-physical being—the core of who we are. This includes mind, emotions, spirit, will, intuition, memory, and the unconscious. The heart encompasses these intangible aspects and is the bodily organ most frequently referred to in the Bible. In both the Hebrew and Christian scriptures, the heart is the place of divine movement where spiritual transformation occurs. God's Spirit is sent into the heart (Gal 4:6). The psalmist prays, "Teach me wisdom in my secret heart" (Ps 51:6). In Jeremiah, the Holy One proclaims, "I will put my law within them, and I will write it on their hearts" (Jer 31:33). Love is poured into the heart through the Holy Spirit

(2 Cor 1:22; Rom 5:5). Christ dwells in the heart and will enlighten the eyes of the heart (Eph 3:1–17).

Throughout this book I refer to the heart as *the authentic* or *true self, deeper self, sanctuary of the soul, secret chamber, the unconscious,* and the *hidden* or *interior realm.* The *unconscious* is the psychological way of speaking about our inner world because it is the area of the unknown. While we do not know or are unaware of what the unconscious contains, this does not lessen its reality. More life and vitality is actually contained in the unconscious than in the conscious or external world. Mystery and wonder inhabit our nonphysical being. Our deepest self lives in this invisible region where hunger for the Beloved resides.

THE PATTERN OF SPIRITUAL TRANSFORMATION

When I open the door of my heart to God, I do more than simply extend a smile of recognition or a nod of welcome. I open myself to grow and change in ways I may never dream likely. I risk being spiritually transformed into a person whose life continually manifests goodness. The pattern of this transformational process parallels the physical movement of going through a doorway. First, I approach the door in order to move beyond where I am now. If the door is closed when I get to it, I open it. Sometimes the door is locked and a key is needed to allow access to the space that lies beyond. As I open the door and prepare to step forward, I move across the threshold, the middle of the doorway. I make a decision about the direction I want to go, either forward or backward across the threshold. With either direction I eventually close the door behind me and move on.

This same type of movement happens on an inner level of myself when life situations and graced moments invite me to become more fully who I am. The choices and decisions I make determine whether I'll go through the door and enter the unknown territory of growth, or turn back and cling to the safety of who I presently am. If I am alert and willing to be transformed, I open the inner door of my self and greet fresh ideas, along with possible changes in attitude and emotional responses. Whenever I choose to open the door and step across the threshold of possibility, I become more conscious of myself as a person with unlimited potential for goodness and ever fuller unity with the divine.

As I reflect upon this pattern of my spiritual journey, I recognize innumerable times when I miss the opportunities that opening a door offers to my spiritual growth. I can be too preoccupied to even notice that the door to growth is there. Sometimes I stop at the door, full of apprehension about continuing onward. Once in a while I keep a door shut that beckons my entrance by refusing to dialogue about a collapsing relationship. Occasionally I linger a long time on the threshold, filled with difficult emotions and wondering about how to take the next step. Often I am nudged across the open doorway by a courageous friend or a wise mentor. Every now and then, life experiences toss me across with such force that I find myself dumped on the other side of the door without having time to make a yes-or-no decision.

What I especially value about the process of spiritual growth is the way the Holy One guides me to explore the inner terrain of my being. Whenever I open the door of my heart and take the passage beyond where I am now, the wonder and richness of divine presence and the resilient beauty of my soul amaze me. As I age, I think I am getting better at deliberately opening the door and leaving the known, safe realms behind. With each threshold crossing, I gain greater freedom to be my most authentic self.

Suggestions for Using This Book

Why this book? How can it help you? How to use it?

THE DOOR TO our heart awaits opening but our fast-paced culture detours us. Unless we set aside intentional time, the door often remains closed. I have arranged this book to provide a structure for you to step aside from your active life and to delve more deeply into your hidden self. I suggest making an appointment with yourself on the calendar for each day of the coming six weeks. Be as responsible to this engagement as you would be with a medical or dental appointment.

You will need twenty to thirty minutes a day to enter into the process of each day's reflection. The time of day makes no difference. Choose what works best for you. This book is designed for six weeks, but do not push yourself to finish in that amount of time. If you need to take longer, do so. If you miss a day or two, be gentle with yourself. Pick up where you left off.

Decide when it works best for you to read the Introduction to each Week. For instance, you might do this the night before you begin the first day of the Week. Start each day's reflection with "A Prayer for Openness" (page 13). Then turn to the day of the week and read the short essay. Ponder the question that follows. You may want to jot down your insights and emotional response to the question. You might not have answers to every question. Perhaps one query will lead to another. Give yourself permission to dwell with what is not yet clear. Let the questions draw you inward, take you deeper.

Read through the meditation and take whatever time you need for this. If the meditation does not suit your manner of praying, adapt it to the form most useful for you. For example, if guided visualization does not appeal to you, or if words get in the way, sit in silence for a while with the Holy One. Conclude with the short prayer given for that particular day.

If you find it helpful, when you leave your place of reflection write the brief scripture verse on an index card. Take it with you and place it where it will remind you of what you reflected on during your prayer time.

You could also choose a door in your home, car, or place of work to remind you to open the door of your heart during these six weeks of intentional reflection. Each time you open or close that door, let it bring you back to the focus of the day.

The seventh day of each week is a day of review and rest. I have designed the weeks this way in order for you to have time to integrate what arises from the reflection and prayer. This will hopefully allow you to feel less pressured to hurry through the days and enable what you have experienced to become more a part of your consciousness.

For those choosing to use this book as a group endeavor, I created a simple structure to use for each week. These group gatherings are in the Appendix. Again, feel free to adapt and change the suggestions to meet the preferences of your group.

As you begin using this book, think of yourself as opening the door to a holy site inside yourself. When you visit this inner realm, I hope the desire to linger there for a considerable amount of time expands for you. I invite you to open (and close) your inner door in order to discover and live more fully your tremendous potential of God-ness. As you reflect and pray, may this process lead you to your authentic self and keep you focused on your ever-evolving transformation.

A Prayer for Openness

Remember the Holy One is with you. Bring to mind this loving presence within you and around you as you pray the following:

1. *Touch your fingertips to your forehead, saying:*
   Open my mind to remember your presence.

2. *Touch your fingertips to your mouth, saying:*
   Open my mouth to speak your wisdom.

3. *Touch your fingertips to your heart, saying:*
   Open my heart to extend your love.

4. *Hold both hands out, open, palms up, saying:*
   Open my hands to serve you generously.

5. *Holding arms wide open, saying:*
   Open my whole being to you.

   Make a deep bow to the loving presence in you.

THE DOOR OF OUR HEART

INTRODUCTION

A door opens in the center of our being
and we seem to fall through it into the immense
depths which, although they are infinite,
are all accessible to us.
—THOMAS MERTON

THE "DOOR" OF our heart is a way of speaking about an invisible passageway through which we enter the endless territory of beauty and truth secluded in our interior world. Unlike the physical doorways we pass through, the door of our heart is hidden. This symbolic door bears a similarity to physical doors in that it, too, opens and closes. Our heartdoor opens inward to the inherent goodness seeded in us at our birth and opens outward to the world where we bring this goodness and share it with others. When we enter the door of our heart and go inward, this nonphysical door allows us to move beyond where we presently are in our beliefs, emotions, attitudes, and actions. By doing so, our spiritual growth evolves and our union with the Holy One matures.

Various sources describe a door as an entrance, opening, passage, and a means of admittance. The door of our heart gives us access to the divine within us and helps us know and accept more of the totality of who we are. While this process goes on repeatedly, we do not always recognize each occurrence. When we do, what a gift it is to experience this revelation. Such an occasion took place for me at dusk on an early June evening.

I sat on the doorstep of my porch, talking on the phone, listening to a newly widowed friend speak of her severe sorrow. In between wrenching tears, she poured out her struggle of attempting to re-engage with a life that no longer included her beloved husband. As I gave full attention to my grieving friend, a young, sleek deer emerged from the woods and stood like a sentinel on the front lawn. At the same time, the tiny lights of fireflies began twinkling in the night air. I felt caught between two contrasting worlds: the sharp pain in my friend's heart and the alluring beauty of the natural world.

Between these two opposites, something unidentified nudged me to pay attention. I let the disparity be there until the phone conversation ended. Then I continued to sit silently on the doorstep, pondering the enticing scene, wondering what stirred inside of me. This movement opened the door to my inner self and led me to look at the part that always wants life to be fair. I recognized my strong desire to relieve my friend of her heartache. At the same time, I also trusted she was in a "growing place" and eventually would be less pained from her loss.

From this pause of reflection, I glimpsed divine presence in both areas: a Compassionate Companion embracing hurting ones and a Generous Creator continually revealing abundant splendor. The deer and the fireflies assured me that beauty remains present in the midst of life's turmoil. That evening the door of my heart provided a passageway to gratitude for enduring beauty and a reminder to trust God's strength to be there, especially when the harshness of life shows its face.

In *The Song of the Seed*, Macrina Wiederkehr's words describe the inner journey I took that night on the doorstep: "Deep within your soul there is a knowing place, a sanctuary. . . . Enter that sacred space." By pausing to reflect, I slipped into my inner sanctuary to tend what drew me inward. If I had ignored my experience of the voice on the phone or the deer and the fireflies on the lawn and simply moved on to other things awaiting me, I would not have visited the truth inside. Because I opened the door by pausing, hope revealed itself.

When I move toward the door to my deeper self and enter into it, I often make connections. It feels like coming home. Newly revealed truth sweeps me out of my boxed-in world and assures me either that things make sense or that acceptance of the situation is the only valid option if I want to grow. While connections take place when I visit the hidden places of my heart, things sometimes fall apart before they come together. Questions, confusions, and distress do not immediately disappear, but eventually, my view of self, God, and life develops a different hue. I receive a more expansive and real look at how to "do" life.

Whenever we are drawn away from our external world toward a focus on our internal one, a door opens and we enter our deeper self. Poet Laureate Stanley Kunitz observed this reality in his memoir, *The Wild Braid*:

> The more you enter into the unconscious life, the more you believe in its existence and know it walks with you, the more available it becomes and the doors open faster and longer. It learns you are a friendly host. It manifests itself instead of hiding from your tyrannical presence. . . .

Oh, that we would become a "friendly host" to the unending treasure in us. This inner world contains landscapes of clarity and rivers of knowledge, shadowed caves with unwanted and unclaimed characteristics waiting to teach us, jewels of wisdom containing strength and guidance, and an air of enticement that forever lures us toward union with our divine Muse.

The Sufi poet Jalaluddin Rumi spoke of this profound reality and urged fathoming the depths of the mysterious self. He lamented that not doing so would be like going to the ocean with its teeming life and only bringing back a pail of water. With the grandeur and opportunity for growth that resides within the ocean of our authentic self, it is surprising that we spend most of our waking life with a focus on the external world. How much richer our life would be if we gave equal time to the internal reality. This realm is always available to us if we are willing to be quiet and attentive long enough to visit it.

This week we seek the door of our heart, which opens to our inner treasures. I encourage you to pause, focus inwardly, take a long gaze at the door of your heart, trust that it can lead you to more than you now know and experience. Notice what this door looks like. See where, to what, and to whom it directs you.

IDENTIFYING THE DOOR

A door is truly an amazing thing.
Closed, it is an agent of separation. . . .
But swing it open and it becomes an invitation,
uniting what before was separate.
—DREW LEDER

THE METAPHOR OF a door provides a symbolic way of identifying who we envision ourselves to be and how we currently experience life. The door also helps us name how we are in relationship with God. Describing what our inner door looks like can be enlightening. A woman at a retreat spoke about her inner door as a "doggie door." She explained that her grief over her son's death was immense, and she could not stand up to get through a large door. Her sorrow brought her down so low emotionally that the only door she felt she could use was, in her words, "one small enough for me to be on my hands and knees."

At another retreat, a young minister eagerly sought insights and skills to deepen his meditation practice. His enthusiasm and unassuming nature inspired me. At the end of the retreat, he thanked me by saying, "You opened some important new doors for me." That metaphor seemed especially appropriate because of his openness and readiness for growth. I had no doubt that his journey with the Holy One would take him into deep and expansive territory.

What does the door of our heart look like? Is it transparent? Can people look through it and find authenticity there? Perhaps the door consists of heavy wood or thick brass. This kind of door might be keeping someone out who needs a welcome, or it could signify strength to live the courage of one's convictions. The door of our heart might be flexible, like a folding door, allowing plenty of space to welcome new growth. The lightness and openness of a screen door might convey easy accessibility to both the inward and outward aspects of one's self. At another time, a revolving door with no direction might best speak to a state of confusion, or a sense of "going around in circles" due to a hectic schedule, or the result of certain personality traits.

Some people have opaque doors. No one can see inside. Others attach padlocks on the door. Perhaps someone hurt them grievously and they fear to trust again. Maybe the door is tightly locked out of concern that someone will gain an entrance and be dismayed at what is found or not found. The door of another heart might be a thin, glass one needing to be carefully opened. Too much pressure or stress, an unplanned or uncontrolled life event, might cause the delicate door to shatter.

Another morsel of information can be elicited by observing the kind of message that hangs on the door of our heart. This note might say something like *Enjoy Your Stay, Room Service, Welcome, Enter at Your Own Risk, Step Inside, Do Not Disturb, No Trespassing,* or *No Longer at this Address.* At an Advent retreat when we painted the symbolic door to our heart, one retreatant put a sign on hers that read: *Wipe Your Feet.* We laughed at that sign, but also recognized the protective message it implied.

The door to our heart can change from day to day, even from hour to hour. My inner door can be transparent. Then something happens to upset me. Maybe I get my credit card statement and see a huge mistake on it. Frustration or concern arises and my door quickly becomes a thick, solid one as I make phone calls to try and protect myself from someone's error or illegal use of my card. Generally, however, the door to our heart bears a certain predominant style until a major change or a definite *attitude adjustment* takes place.

As you ponder what type of door most symbolizes your current view of yourself and your life with God, let these words of Jeanette Winterson's novel *Lighthousekeeping* remind you of the mystery and wonder of who you are:

You are the door in the rock that finally swings free when the moonlight shines on it. You are the door at the top of the stairs that only appears in dreams. You are the door that sets prisoners free. You are the carved low door into the Chapel of the Grail. You are the door at the edge of the world. You are the door that opens onto a sea of stars.

REFLECT ON THE FOLLOWING:

What kind of door is the door of your heart? Does this door assist or hinder your spiritual growth?

MEDITATION

After you decide what kind of door most symbolizes yourself, take some deep breaths. Settle into a peaceful posture. Close your eyes and visualize your door. Imagine that the Holy One comes and opens this door. Welcome this beloved visitor with as much fullness of your heart as you can. Remain in the peaceful and reassuring presence of the Holy One for a while. Conclude with any other communication you wish to have with your divine companion, and then go forth to bless life with your goodness. (You might want to draw the door that symbolizes yourself and give it a name.)

PRAYER

Companion of my growth,
many are the turns and tumbles
of my ever-changing life.
As I find my way on the journey
of spiritual transformation,
I trust that your abiding presence
will guide and guard me.
I open the door of my heart to you.
I open the door.

Do you not know that you are God's temple and that God's Spirit dwells in you? (1 Cor 3:16).

WEEK 1, DAY 2

THE DOOR OF DIVINITY

So, again Jesus said to them,
"Very truly, I tell you, I am the gate. . . ."
—JOHN 10:7

IN SOME RELIGIOUS traditions, "gate" and "door" are used interchangeably to speak about a divine being. The Hebrew scriptures picture Holy Wisdom sitting by the gates of the city ready to welcome those who approach. "Happy is the one who listens to me, watching daily at my gates, waiting beside my doors" (Prv 8:34). Buddha's disciples quote their enlightened teacher as saying, "I am the Door." The Sufis of Islam refer to Allah as "The Opener and the Closer" of doors. In John's gospel, Jesus announces that he is the "gate" or "door" to fullness of life (Jn 10:9–10).

If we look at what a physical door does, use of this image to connect with the sacred becomes apparent. A physical door is a means of access to another space. The divine door is also an accessible passage, opening the way for us to explore the mysterious regions of our true self. The Holy One offers safe, protective passage, whether we roam in the hitherto unknown regions of our soul or move about in the external world exploring life from its diverse angles. Day by day, we continually pass through the Door of Love.

The story of the Exodus journey exemplifies the door of divinity as a conduit for spiritual growth. When the Israelites hurried away from enslavement in Egypt, they brought with them an unquenchable thirst for a homeland of their own. The Door of Love provided access for them to move toward this goal. The Exodus people experienced this door each day of their long, tedious journey to the promised land. The Great Door never closed to this people bound together by a desire for liberation. God's heart remained ajar in spite of their doubts, grumblings, hesitations, and rebellions. As they passed through the wilderness, these wanderers were nourished, forgiven, challenged, taught, guided, and transformed by this faithful Presence.

Each encounter moved the wandering people farther along toward the promised land, even though they were never sure if they would arrive there. The Exodus community kept entering the passageway of growth, learning from their failures and their increasingly purified faith. Always, the divine door provided both protection and clearance for what lay ahead in their search for a home.

This group of people wandering through their unfolding life represents the soul of each person searching for the promised land of personal authenticity and a vibrant life with God. Here, too, the Holy One becomes the door, providing safe passage and clearance to what lies ahead in the journey to wholeness. The Door of Divinity is a channel of love, constantly available for us to pass through as we enter our chamber of transformation. As we continue this journey throughout our lifetime, the Door of Divinity always stands open as a grace-filled passageway.

A long time ago I heard a professor in a spirituality class warn, "Be sure to take God with you when you go within." In other words, "Be sure you pass through the Great Door of Love as you enter the realm of your deeper self" so you do not dismiss, deny, or dodge anything that seeks your attention when you enter the depths of your being. Like the Israelites, if we forget or ignore the Door of Love, doubts and discouragement easily overpower us.

As with the Exodus people traveling through unfamiliar and sometimes treacherous territory, when we enter unknown terrain, some encounters will threaten to detour us from our path of spiritual growth. We can find ourselves grumbling when life does not give us all we want or when the price of transformation costs us dearly. Failures, defeats, and disillusionments temporarily wipe out our hope of reaching the promised land of our true self until we realize these very experiences are stepping-stones to the wisdom we need. Just about the time we get fed up with our wandering and seeming lack of direction, we remember we have safe passage in the One who is our constant guide. All we need do is turn ourselves toward the Great Door, move through this conduit of love, and travel peacefully again.

Now is the time to remember the Exodus journeys of your life and revisit what you learned from them. Look back and see how the Great Door provided a passageway for you to further freedom.

Reflect on the following:

How has God been a door in your life?

Meditation

Allow yourself to enter into stillness. Set aside disruptive thoughts and feelings. Gently let your body, mind, and spirit sink into peaceful repose. Imagine you are passing through the door of God's love. Sense this protective care surrounding you. Look ahead through the open door and notice the welcoming space before you. See the path that beckons. Take a deep breath and receive the strength, guidance, and safety the divine door provides as you prepare to continue on your journey of life. Rest quietly with this reassurance. Close your meditation by renewing your trust in the Great Door and the openness available to you.

Prayer

Great Door of Love,
assure me of your protective presence
as I wander about the landscape of my life.
When I become lost, clear a path for hope.
May every seeking footstep of mine
take me through the doorway of your love.
Be my passageway today. O, be my passageway.
I open the door of my heart to you.

I open the door.

Happy is the one who listens to me, watching daily at my gates, waiting beside my doors (Prv 8:34).

WEEK 1, DAY 3

KEYS TO THE DOOR

Asking the proper question is the central action
of transformation. . . .
Questions are the keys that cause
the secret doors of the psyche to swing open.
—CLARISSA PINKOLA ESTÉS

CERTAIN DOORS THAT we use each day, like those of our home, need a key to unlock them. The same is true with our inner world. There, too, the door requires unlocking before we gain entrance. "Anyone of us can, at any time, enter the house of God. All we have to do is turn the key," comments spiritual teacher, J. P. Vaswani. How true this is and, yet, how challenging at times to find the key that opens the way to the house of divinity within us.

Drew Leder, author of *Sparks of the Divine,* reflects on the nature of keys:

> . . . The particular serrations and angles that release a key-lock are hidden inside, invisible, leaving us excluded and baffled. . . . Sometimes things feel like that. We reach for what to say to an angry spouse, what shifts need to be made in a marriage. More honesty? Or tactfulness? More self-assertion or less? More time

and activities apart, or more togetherness? We flip through the keys, but cannot tell which one will release the recalcitrant lock.... Still, we persist. If we are sincere in our efforts—if in our actions we manifest willingness to change—if in our humility, we consult with others and with God, the master Locksmith—we are likely to finally find the key.

Leder reminds us that persistence, sincerity, a willingness to change, communication with others and with God are essential in helping us locate the keys to our inner chamber. Provocative questions are some of the best keys for opening the inner door, especially when we feel stuck, unable, or unwilling to enter this hidden realm. Stimulating questions bring us to attention and draw us beyond our present responsiveness, awakening us to how we are to grow. We can be quite sure a question has acted as a key when it urges us to move into untraveled territory or to revisit that which has escaped our awareness.

A single inquiry can act like an arrow going straight to the heart of the matter. Dawna Markova asks these sorts of questions in *I Will Not Die an Unlived Life*. Three of her queries especially draw me inward:

> What is it too soon for, too late for, just the right time for?
> When you are very still in a place without words, steeped in silence, when the world is elsewhere with its noise and motion, what are the sacred hungers that echo inside of you?
> Who am I when I stop doing?

When questions act as keys for opening the door of our heart, they do not necessarily provide answers, nor should we always expect this result. Rather, these questions point us in a certain direction. They propel us inward where we elicit further information for clarification or take another step toward the direction of inner freedom. "True guides... are filled with wisdom but are not answer people," notes Robert Wicks. "Instead, they call us to live with the questions in a different way.... So, rather than being answer people true guides move us away from the habit of believing quick answers are the most ideal steps to living fully." And yet, how desperately we want answers and want them *now*. If only we could believe and trust that the questions themselves have tremendous worth.

Thought-provoking questions are keys for opening the door to a deeper life with God. Like true guides, they may not give us immediate answers, but they enable us to identify and face unknown or unresolved aspects of our spiritual life. If we are to grow, we must also be willing to ask penetrating questions of our deepest self and be ready to give them due attention.

As Dawna Markova so wisely writes: "May we all find the courage we need to ask ourselves the questions that will free our minds and strengthen our souls."

REFLECT ON THE FOLLOWING:

What is the central question of your life right now?

MEDITATION

Take the question of your life with you as you enter into meditation. Begin by recalling that you are not alone. The Holy One is with you. Open your mind and heart to this peaceful presence. Take the question you have identified and bring it to the Holy One. What thoughts and feelings arise as you sit with the question? Are there clarifications? More questions? A sense of direction? Write the responses down. Return your focus to the presence of divine peace within you. Resolve to carry this peace with you as you depart from your meditation.

PRAYER

Opener of Hearts,
you are the true guide of my life
helping me unlock every door that leads to you.
As I move amid the mystery of myself,
I seek to know your desires for my growth.
Keep showing me the way to you
as I turn to you with trust and with faith.
I open the door of my heart to you.
I open the door.

When you search for me, you will find me; if you seek me with all your heart (Jer 29:13).

WEEK 1, DAY 4

THE CONCEALED DOOR

There are people whose presence is encouraging. . . .
The sense of encouragement you feel from them is not
simply their words or gestures; it is rather their whole
presence enfolding you and helping you find the
concealed door.
—JOHN O'DONOHUE

THE SECRET GARDEN is one of my favorite books. In this hope-filled story, ten-year-old orphaned Mary is sent to live with her reclusive uncle in the desolate Yorkshire moors. As she goes about her daily explorations, she finds a high-walled garden. Mary longs to get inside that garden but she cannot find the entrance into it. The walls are covered with thick, dangling vines due to years of neglect, and they hide the wooden gate. Day after day Mary goes back to the garden, bringing with her a constant yearning to find a way inside.

One sunny day a chirping robin flits from the top of the garden wall to the ground beside her. Mary looks down to where the bird has landed and sees the top of a buried key. Not long after she digs the rusty key out, Mary discovers the concealed gate. Her heart beats wildly as she turns the corroded key in the lock. One strong turn, a bit of grunting effort to push the long unused gate open, and Mary is finally able to walk into the abandoned garden. Eventually, with the assistance of some newly found friends, Mary restores the place to its natural beauty.

In many ways, our hidden self is like the secret garden Mary found. We have this realm of beauty and potential growth within us, but we do not always believe in it or know how to reach it. When we do find our way to our true self, there is work to be done in order to resurrect or restore our innate goodness. Anne Lamott describes her inner garden this way:

> If my heart were a garden, it would be in bloom with roses and wrinkly Indian poppies and wild flowers. There would be two unmarked tracts of scorched earth, and scattered headstones covered with weeds and ivy and moss, a functioning compost pile, great tangles of blackberry bushes, and some piles of trash I've meant to haul away for years.

Like Mary's robin and the friends who assisted her, we, too, have helpers in our life who knowingly or unknowingly aid us in our search for the concealed door to our inner garden. Who are these companions of growth? Mine have been people who believed in me before I believed in myself. Sometime ago I read a novel by Joan Ohanneson about the German mystic, Hildegard of Bingen. I remember well one line from it: "But my daughter, the abbess' trust in you is the key that opens the gate." My companions of growth have been diverse, but all have had one common characteristic: each trusted in my potential for growth. I never would have found the key to my inner garden had they not believed in the possibilities yet to come alive in my undeveloped self.

These companions challenged me to see the parts of my self that were encumbered by my ego. They gave me courage to seek and find the veiled realm of my authentic self. Book reviewer David Davies writes: ". . . Insights into our own shadows are best gained in the company of others who lovingly offer us their vision from vantage points not blocked by the pillars of our own ego."

The sum of all this is that others can help us open the door of our heart. We need them to teach us how to pray, to encourage us to find and use our personal talents, to challenge us to expand our minds and hearts, to assure our efforts. Rarely do we grow spiritually entirely on our own. Each of us benefits enormously by having someone trust in us and believe in our secret garden when we are not so sure it exists, or when we question its potential for growth. It is to our benefit that these teachers and supporters urge us onward as we probe the secret regions of our self and bring our neglected or newly discovered gifts into being.

Whether these companions of growth are persons we know and admire or strangers who enter our life for a brief stay through their trusted presence and teachings, they lead us to those secret places where the seeds of our inner garden wait to be born.

Why not open a concealed door to your heart and visit your inner garden today?

REFLECT ON THE FOLLOWING:

Who are the significant people who helped you find the concealed door to your deeper self?

MEDITATION

Light a candle. Place it on the floor in the center of an open doorway. Sit by the candle. Look back in memory to those who have been a light for your journey, those who helped you find your way to the garden inside. Think about how you have grown because of their presence. Offer thanks for what you have received. As you blow out the candle, resolve to be a supportive presence for others who seek to find the concealed door to their inner garden.

PRAYER

Trusted Gardener,
tame what has grown too wild.
Free what has become too tame.
Claim what has been neglected.
Awaken what has been dormant.
Thank you for the companions
whose presence led me to my deeper self.

I open the door of my heart to you.
I open the door of my heart.

SCRIPTURE TO CARRY IN YOUR HEART TODAY:
. . . that we may be mutually encouraged by each other's faith . . .
(Rom 1:12).

WEEK 1, DAY 5

WALLS PRETENDING TO BE DOORS

Then there were doors that wouldn't open
unless you asked politely,
or tickled them in exactly the right place,
and doors that weren't really doors at all,
but solid walls just pretending.
—J.K. ROWLING

THE MAGICAL WORLD of Hogwarts where Harry Potter goes to school contains a zillion secret doors. In *The Sorcerer's Stone*, Harry rushes along to his destination but the doors he tries to open turn out to be walls that refuse to let him pass. The place is filled with illusions. Like Harry Potter's supposed doors, there are times when what we think is the door leading to our authentic self turns out to be a wall of illusion blocking our journey of spiritual transformation.

Solid walls are not doors. Illusions are not legitimate reality. What we believe about some part of our self is not always as it seems. Although illusions appear to be doors to greater growth, they actually keep us from our genuine self. Illusions convince us that our views and actions are serving our growth well and that we do not need to change. These illusions assure us that it makes no difference if we have more truth in our life. They keep us stuck in our false self by trying to persuade us away from whatever our further development necessitates.

Illusions are "pretend doors." The counterfeit self is filled with these masquerades. These pretenders deceive us into thinking our motivation or behavior opens us up when they actually close us off like a wall.

Here are some illusions I've noticed in myself and others:

- pretending to be a caring door of compassion yet resisting the precious time it takes to listen to another person's suffering;
- pretending to be an open door of friendship while exerting control over the relationship with subtle demands or jealous requirements;
- pretending to be a door of humility, but actually being fearful of accepting or using the undeveloped and unrecognized talents within one's self;
- pretending to be a door of trust in God, yet anxious and worried whenever things do not go as planned or hoped;
- pretending to enjoy the achievements of others while envying and desiring their spiritual growth or professional success;
- pretending to be a door of gratitude, but feeling entitled to every opportunity and gift that presents itself;
- pretending to be a door of forgiveness while harboring hateful feelings for someone whose words and actions sliced like a knife;
- pretending to love one's self, yet continually giving in to mental put-downs and emotions that perpetuate a lack of self-esteem.

One of the ways I get in touch with my illusions is by listening to my "gut responses." When I feel strong resistance and irritability, or sense myself wanting to defend my mental positions and emotional postures due to the words and actions of others, I am quite sure an old wall of illusion needs to be toppled. When I have the courage to tend to these resistances and let go of my illusions of supposed truth, I tickle the door to new growth, and the passageway to greater inner freedom springs opens.

As you near the close of this week in which you have reflected on the door of your heart, the opportunity to discover more of your true self awaits you. Listen well to how you think and feel today. Pay attention to any resistances. Genuine Love will help you recognize what is a solid wall pretending to be a door and what is truly an opening to continued transformation. Look at your life with an honest and heartfelt desire to be your authentic self.

Reflect on the following:

Is there a solid wall in your life pretending to be an open door?

Meditation

Stand next to a solid wall. Push with both hands on this wall. Notice how you cannot budge the wall. Then take your hands off the wall and sit down for your meditation. Place your hands over your heart. Pray to have any inner walls of resistance made known. Be still and do not force any insights or feelings. Let whatever comes present itself to you. Pay attention to your gut response when thoughts and feelings arise. Remember, God is the one who can help you recognize your illusions. Ask for what you need. Renew your desire for spiritual growth and confidently place yourself in the Holy One's care before you close this meditation time.

Prayer

Truth-Bearer,
I desire to know the illusions
that keep me from growing.
Help me pay attention to what stirs within me.
May any falseness in my life be revealed.
Lead me to the peaceful place deep within
where you and I are truly one.
I open the door of my heart to you.
I open the door.

Scripture to carry in your heart today:

Lead me in your truth, and teach me (Ps 25:5).

THE DOOR TO GROWTH

This passage is a doorway for you—
keep it alive and keep it vital with meaning.
—JOHN MILTON

AS I WAS writing this book, I invited visitors to my website to submit stories about doors they had either read about or personally experienced. One of the most profound submissions came from the mother of a twelve-year-old daughter. This child, Mary Katherine Lidle, wrote the following untitled poem on the night before she was struck by an automobile in 1982. The accident was on March 17 and she died on March 25. Her poem contains immense wisdom regarding our journey of spiritual growth. Read it first from the precious heart of a twelve-year-old. Then, re-read it as a lesson for your own heart.

> Look at me—
> I'm walking through a door
> My life is changing and it's just perfect now
> No more doors for me
> They're too hard to get through
> I'm staying here where it's safe—
> No, child,
> Those doors are a part of you
> You can't ignore them
> 'Cause they're there
> You've got to go through them
> Who knows what you'll find
> You've got to meet their trial
> If you don't, you won't be what you should become
> There are always gonna be doors and you
> Can't stop 'em from comin'

You've got to go through them to grow
It's called change
Look at the wildflower; it changes all the time
always blossoming or closing up, sprouting or withering
You're scared to go through those doors
Into the unknowing, "into change"
You don't know what's going to happen
You don't know what change is going to bring
Listen to me
Go through those doors with hope
Go through those doors knowing change is the future
and you're part of it
You don't know what change is, that's why
you're scared
Change is the sun booming over the horizon
Scattering rays of hope to a new day
Change is a baby lamb meeting the world for its first time
Change is growing from a young child to a young woman
Change is beautiful; you will learn to love it

—MARY KATHERINE LIDLE

In her short twelve years of life, Mary Katherine captured the basic truth about change: we've got to give ourselves to it. Growth will not happen without moving on from who we now are. We ought not to fear change but, rather, welcome and embrace it. All forms of life require alteration. Without regular adaptation, life stagnates and dies. This includes the spiritual life. Each day God calls us to stretch a little further, search a little deeper, and become a little freer. Let us "go through those doors with hope" as she suggests, accepting the inevitability of change and trusting in its benefits for our transformation.

REFLECT ON THE FOLLOWING:
What door of change are you currently going through?

MEDITATION

Read the story of Mary, mother of Jesus, and her struggle to go through the door of change (Lk 1:26–38). Notice how she struggled and questioned before she was able to leave behind the life she had known and presumed would be hers. Ponder how Mary went forth through the door of faith. Reflect on her trust in the Holy One. Turn, then, to your own door of change. Focus on your faith and trust in God. With what do you struggle? What brings you peace and acceptance? Close by giving your heart to the One who invites you to ever fuller communion.

PRAYER

Trusted Companion of my journey,
you call me to go through doors of change.
Turn my wavering heart toward you.
Teach me to trust in your guidance.
Convince me of the benefits of change.
Deepen my belief in possibilities of growth.
Most of all, strengthen my love for you.
I open the door of my heart to you.
I open the door.

SCRIPTURE TO CARRY IN YOUR HEART TODAY:

You will show me the path of life. In your presence there is fullness of joy (Ps 16:11).

WEEK 1, DAY 7

REVIEW AND REST

THIS IS YOUR day to gather what has taken place for you during the past week of using this book. It is also meant to be a day of rest for you. Let this reflection and integration time be a gentle pause in your week.

(You might choose to read the Introduction to the next week's prayer in the evening of this day or wait and begin fresh the next day, reading it at that time.)

Begin

"A Prayer for Openness" (page 13).

Review

Look back over the week. If you wrote in your journal, review what you've written. If you did not write, sit quietly for a few minutes and let your reflections from this week visit you. Then, respond in writing to the following:

1. The most helpful part of the past week's reflection and prayer was . . .
2. The most challenging part of the past week's reflection and prayer was . . .
3. I want to remember . . .
4. I hope that . . .
5. I wonder . . .

Complete your reflection with a one- or two-line summary of your experience from the week. An alternative to writing might be to summarize the week by drawing, sculpting, creating music, dancing, or using some other form of alternative expression to gather and integrate the week's experience into your present situation.

Another alternative to writing would be to summarize each week by drawing a door. Place words, phrases, drawings, or other symbols on the door to depict what happened within the week to draw you into further growth. (Instead of drawing a door, you could post these words, etc., on a real door in your home.)

Conclude

Close with one of the prayers from the week and/or by sitting quietly for a few minutes of gratitude.

Week 2

Knocking on the Door

INTRODUCTION

Listen! I am standing at the door, knocking;
if you hear my voice and open the door,
I will come in to you and eat with you,
and you with me.

—REVELATION 3:20

KNOCKING AT A door requires more physical exertion than ringing a doorbell. Perhaps that is why knocking on a door is an apt metaphor when speaking about an attentive heart. Spiritual growth requires energy. Recognition and acceptance of our true self results when we are intentional about the endeavor and extend a wholehearted response to the process of transformation.

In the introduction to this book, I refer to Warner Sallman's painting in which he shows Jesus knocking, waiting for the door to be opened. Here is one of numerous paradoxes in the spiritual life. In John's gospel, Jesus describes *himself* as a door. In the Book of Revelation he is depicted as *standing* at the door. In Revelation the door refers to *us,* to our heart. Let's take a detailed look at Revelation 3:20 because this scriptural passage contains rich insight regarding spiritual transformation.

I AM STANDING . . .

A colleague of mine remarked that she feels more power and energy when she stands to speak before a group than when she sits. Standing is a posture of strength. However, standing becomes a posture of vulnerability when one waits before a closed door, knocking in hope of being let in. Much depends on what takes place on the opposite side of the closed door. The waiting person wonders: Is anyone home? Will the knock at the door be heard? Ignored? Who will come to the door? What kind of welcome will take place? When Christ stands at the door of our hearts, similar questions arise in regard to how we will respond: Will we open the door or not? What will happen if we do?

KNOCKING . . .

When someone knocks at the door of our home, it might be a loud rap, a strong thump, a steady beat, a gentle tap, or an angry, persistent pounding. The kind of knock reflects both the type of personality and the emotional state, as well as the reason for coming to the door. While the way Christ knocks at our heart's door also varies, the knock carries a central message: "Open up! Let me enter your life. Each part of it. I will guide you to what benefits your growth."

At times, a little tap from the divine gets our attention like the sight of a bluebird calling us to joy. At other times a persistent rapping is the only way to move us to open up. Such is the case of a woman who told me about a book she felt she was meant to read, but thought she was too busy to do. One day she saw the book on a store shelf. As she took it down and browsed through it, she became even more sure she would read it "sometime." She put the book back on the shelf and began to walk away. The book fell onto the floor. She picked it up and put it back on the shelf. As she walked away a second time, again the book fell onto the floor. She picked it up and put it back once more. This time as she started to walk away, the book fell out and bonked her on the head. She finally got the message, bought the book, and found it to contain exactly the wisdom she sought.

IF YOU HEAR . . .

Hearing the knock is crucial for us if we intend to open the door. Esther de Waal notes how vital it is to clear out and quiet ourselves in order to heed the knock.

> In the complex of my own daily schedule, with all its demands, I am reminded that it is important, and more than that, fundamental and essential, to keep clear, open space in my own heart. This means in spite of all the demands, the distractions, and the difficulties that besiege my time, I shall try to carry a heart of stillness.

We will not be able to hear the Holy One's knock if our heart contains disruptive noise. Silence and deliberate solitude enable us to be aware of a presence larger than ourselves within the pulsating rhythm of our full days. Without some tranquility and deliberate effort to quiet the rush of our inner and outer self, we miss what calls us to wholeness.

MY VOICE . . .

Author Bill Huebsch writes: "Deep within us, I found, there is a voice, ever calling us to love and to do what is good and avoid what is not. That voice sounds in our hearts at the right moment. For we have in our hearts a voice inscribed by God." This voice of divinity resounds in each moment of life, providing us greater clarity, urging us to be who we are meant to be. The voice of Holy Wisdom offers guidance and direction, welcomes the lost, comforts the grieving, chides the wayward, encourages the forsaken, and "compassionates" those broken in body and spirit.

I WILL COME IN AND EAT WITH YOU, AND YOU WITH ME . . .

On the day I paid close attention to Revelation 3:20, I heard a news report on National Public Radio about an experiment related to food. The person conducting the research went to various restaurants. At each one he asked strangers seated at the table next to him if he could have a bite of their food to see how it tasted. Amazingly, almost every stranger offered him a morsel of something. Conversation and camaraderie among the strangers and himself invariably followed his tasting their food.

This news report confirmed the old adage that dining together can be an intimate act. Sharing food offers the possibility of bringing people closer together. This communion and bonding is the promise and assurance of Revelation 3:20. Those who open the door of their heart experience a communion both nourishing and transforming.

This week focuses on awareness and response to the Holy One's presence. I invite you to be attentive and alert to how the Indwelling One knocks on the door of your heart. Notice how you respond. I also encourage you to reflect on how you knock on the divine one's heart and what you expect when the door is opened to you.

WEEK 2, DAY 1

KNOCKING ON EVERY DOOR

The traveler has to knock at every
alien door to come to his own.
—RABINDRANATH TAGORE

TAGORE'S WORDS REMIND me of a legend found in various lands. No matter what ethnicity or language, the tale contains similar features about a person who has an enticing dream of where treasure is located. Of course, the valuable cache in the dream hides far beyond where the person lives. If the dreamer does not leave home to seek the treasure, the dream is repeated until the person finally sets out for the extensive journey. In each legend, the seeker travels long, arduous years, filled with both dangerous and enthralling adventure, never being sure if that which is sought will be found.

The story ends with the traveler coming to the place where the treasure is supposedly hidden. Instead of finding it there, the seeker meets a stranger at that site who tells about a dream he or she had in which the long-sought treasure is located back at the place where the dreamer originally started out. Of course, the person who has been seeking all those years now hurries as quickly as possible to get home. Arriving back at the place of the dream, sure enough, there is the treasure. What the person sought on the arduous journey had been there all along.

This legend teaches that life's journey, with its flow of ups and downs, has to be made. Although it leads full circle back to the home of one's own heart, the journey itself contains the necessary teachings for growth and change. The treasure in our heart will not be found without each person, place, and experience along life's path. The journey is lengthy. There is much to learn. Each step on the way offers meaning and direction, bringing us into our deep self where the finest treasure awaits discovery. The ancient sage Silvanus encouraged this kind of journeying.

> Knock upon yourself as upon a door, and walk upon yourself as on a straight road. For if you walk on that path, you cannot go astray; and when you knock on that door, what you open for yourself shall open.

Each of us is a traveler of the heart. As we traverse the road of life, we come to unknown and unsought doors revealing further truth about our authentic self. These unfamiliar doors of life hide pieces of beneficial wisdom. They contain information for our transformation even though we may not understand this for quite a while. Some alien doors, upon first glance, do not seem worthy enough to be catalysts, appearing either too painful or too mundane to serve as sources of truth. Certain people or events definitely do not fit the picture of how we think we are to be aided in our spiritual growth.

The experiences of life frequently divert us rather than bring us directly to our inner treasure, causing us to doubt their worth. Each step of the way holds another opportunity for knowing who we are and how we are to live. Those things that seem foreign to our purpose, that seem unworthy of being a source of growth or make no sense at the time, are the very doors to be knocked on and entered. Rabbi Lawrence Kushner points this out:

> Holy gates are everywhere. . . . Culture and organized religion conspire to trick us into believing that entrances to holiness are only at predictable times and prearranged places. . . . Entrances to holiness are everywhere and all the time.

Like the legend of the treasure, life is a parable carrying messages about our inner richness. Every moment is a doorway, a promise of revelation. Doors to the sacred are waiting for our knock. If we give due attention and do not run from what repels or brings us pain, we unearth a wealth of knowledge and inspiration. We find our way home.

Today I encourage you to knock on the door of your life even though you may not want what the door reveals. Knock when there is grief behind the door, when there is anger, confusion, disgust, criticism, or utter silence. Knock when there is affirmation, amazement, and consolation. Never doubt that each particle of life, no matter how mundane, dramatic, painful, pleasurable, or simple, has a door awaiting your opening.

REFLECT ON THE FOLLOWING:

What is the unwanted piece of your life, the "alien door," that waits for you to knock and seek entrance?

MEDITATION

Sit quietly. Gradually move into the deeper part of yourself. As you go within, the Holy One takes you by the hand. Allow yourself to be led to a door you would rather ignore. When you come to this door, turn to the Holy One. Receive the assurance and strength you need to knock on the door. After you knock, let the door open. With your hand in the Holy One's, pass through the doorway. Look around inside. Listen. Is there a teaching or a message waiting for you? When you sense it is time, return back. Sit quietly as you ponder what this experience means to you. Close with a prayer of hope.

PRAYER

Trusted and Wise Companion,
remind me often that you accompany me.
You are near as I walk through each part
of the great circle I call my life.
You guide me lovingly as I go on my way,
as I seek the treasure hidden within my depths.
Strengthen and renew my hope daily.
I open the door of my heart to you.
I open the door.

Be strong and courageous . . . your God is with you wherever you go (Jos 1:9).

WEEK 2, DAY 2

LISTENING FOR THE KNOCK

When a moment knocks on the door of your life,
it is often no louder than the beating of your heart,
and it is very easy to miss it.
—BORIS PASTERNAK

LIFE CONTAINS CONTINUOUS wake-up calls, alerting us to the moments that reveal another dimension of our true self. How will we hear these opportunities for growth unless we are vigilant? Healthy spirituality includes interior and exterior attentiveness. This alertness requires listening. Paying attention would seem to be one of the easier tasks of the spiritual life, but reality contradicts this presumption. If anything, listening becomes ever more challenging because of the clamor and burdens of our hurried days. Poet Laureate Ted Kooser remarks, "What seems like a simple discipline turns out to be quite difficult because, by habit, most of us go through our lives without paying much attention to anything."

This inability to be vigilant and attentive is not only a cultural problem, but also a human inclination. Long ago, Jesus chose to teach about alertness through the parable of the wedding banquet in which the servants are waiting for the head of the household to return: "Be like those who are waiting for their master to return from the wedding banquet, so that they may open the door for him as soon as he comes and knocks" (Lk 12:36).

Numerous scriptural passages also encourage listening. God speaks to Job, "Listen to me; be silent, and I will teach you wisdom" (Jb 33:33). In *The Book of Proverbs*, Holy Wisdom urges: "And now, my children, listen to me" (Prv 8:32). An especially beautiful description of devoted listening and consequent openness comes forth from the mouth of the lover in The Song of Solomon: "I slept but my heart was awake. Listen! my beloved is knocking. 'Open to me . . .'" (Sg 5:2).

Such keen vigilance! How wonderful to have our heart be that "awake." Illness, depression, certain personality traits, overwhelming home and work responsibilities prevent us from a focused awareness. Being busy in itself is not a dreadful thing, but becomes a major stumbling block to our readiness to listen when it keeps us from being alert and responsive.

This is why listening is to be cultivated and renewed each day. Our lives are too full and active to automatically allow for a natural flow of attentiveness. We cannot run through life and expect that we will hear what stirs deep within us or notice what begs our attention without regularly adjusting our listening antennae. God is present to us in the scriptures, the liturgical life of the church, our work, prayer, people, events, and nature. Not a person, place, or a moment is left out from divine revelation. Something of value for our growth is always being made known to us in the midst of our ordinary lives. This revelation stretches far beyond and much deeper than how we usually perceive life. Our spiritual development depends on our being alive and vigilant enough to hear the message of transformation that weaves through our daily existence.

Cardinal Basil Hume of England suggests taking deliberate pauses of quiet to develop and maintain this essential vigilance:

> Each of us needs an opportunity to be alone, and silent, to find space in the day or in the week, just to reflect and to listen to the voice of God that speaks deep within us. Our search for God is only our response to [God's] search for us. [God] knocks at our door, but for many people their lives are too preoccupied for them to be able to hear.

Let this day be one of a renewed desire to open the door of your heart. No matter how full this day might be for you, be intentional about this desire.

REFLECT ON THE FOLLOWING:

What most distracts and keeps you from listening to the deeper part of your life?

MEDITATION

Begin by paying attention to your breathing. Simply notice the breath coming in, going out. Now focus on your sense of hearing. Listen to each and every sound around you: the hum of machines, music, voices, traffic, children . . . and, if you are fortunate enough, the sound of silence. Simply sit and listen as intently as you can. Now close your eyes and open the door of your heart. Listen to the presence of Love within your inner chamber. Be at peace. (I encourage you to do this meditation at least three times today. It can be done anywhere, anytime.)

PRAYER

O Blessed Presence,
how is it that you are forever faithful
to my wandering self?
How is it that you linger lovingly
no matter how inattentive I may be?
Turn my heart toward your love
again and again and again.
I open the door of my heart to you.
I open the door.

SCRIPTURE TO CARRY IN YOUR HEART TODAY:

I slept, but my heart was awake.
Listen! my beloved is knocking (Sg 5:2).

THE DOOR SHALL BE OPENED

So I say to you, Ask, and it will be given you;
search, and you will find;
knock, and the door will be opened for you.
—LUKE 11:9

WHEN DO WE knock on the divine door? Certainly in our formal prayer and worship, but also in our informal prayer. Each time we turn our heart in trust toward our Constant Companion and acknowledge our need of divine assistance, we are knocking on the door. As the years of our prayer unfold, one truth becomes ever more convincing: we cannot do our life without divine guidance.

What is it we are to ask for when we come to the divine door and knock? Jesus encourages his followers to be deliberate about searching and requesting. He promises they will find what they are seeking. The assumption has been made by many that Jesus is talking about intercessory prayer, the container of those big and little things we petition God for each day to help make life go the way we want it to go. Perhaps this is so. But could it be that Jesus was speaking not so much about our external world as our internal one? Could he have meant knocking and searching for what will enhance the relationship of love that flows like a river between the Holy One and our self? Are we to knock on the door and ask for what enriches and enlivens this bond? Are we to request mainly what nurtures this union?

Jesus promises we will receive if we knock on the door. What is it that we will receive? After we make our appeal, will we gain what most aids our spiritual well-being? Could it be the response comes disguised as a gift requiring patience and faith to receive? Might it be that the divine response is more generous than we ever anticipated? Is every reply bestowed with full consideration as to what is most vital for our interior life?

It seems to me that when Jesus urges us to knock on the door and assures us we will receive, we are to ask for what matures and strengthens our relationship with the divine. We are to request what will transform us into our best gladness, our firmest faithfulness, our strongest fire. We are to petition what will prepare us to be catalysts of goodness in our world. The foundational message of Jesus centers on the indispensable gift of love, a love that grows deep, tall, strong, and enduring, a love meant to be shared. Could we ask for anything less?

Irish singer Carmel Boyle created a lovely piece of music titled "My Soul's Desire." In this song, she asks some central questions related to spiritual transformation. Each response made to these questions points toward the true nature of our requests when we knock on the divine door:

> What is your longing?
> What is your hope?
> What is your yearning?
>
> What is your song?
> What is your calling?
> What is your hurt?
> What is your healing?
> What is your joy?
> What is your wisdom?
> What is your truth?
> What is your freedom?
> What is your fire?

As we ask these questions of ourselves, our petitions at God's door might become not so much "What can you *do* for me?" as "Who can you *be* for me?" There is so much the Holy One can be for us: the mentor of our loving, the source of our courage, the keeper of our troubles, the teacher of our prayer, the guide of our pathway, the nurturer of our virtue, the companion of our soul.

When you knock on the divine door today, think about what your requests have been in the past and what they might be now. Will you ask for what helps you develop your authentic self?

Reflect on the following:

What is the deepest desire of your heart? For what are you searching and hoping to find?

Meditation

Close your eyes and visualize a door. Imagine yourself knocking on this door. When the door is opened, you find Jesus or another form of divinity before you. Hear the invitation to come inside. Go within and let yourself be welcomed with joyful hospitality. Turn now to this divine figure and speak about the deepest desire of your heart. Listen to the response you receive. As your meditation comes to a close, hold what you most want to remember near to your heart. After this, offer thanks and receive a warm, strong embrace before you depart.

Prayer

Beloved One,
you know my heart through and through.
Your gaze penetrates to the core of who I am,
where the truest and deepest of my desire dwells.
When I knock on your door with my requests,
grant what will most influence my love for you.
May I ever seek that which you long for me to be.
I open the door of my heart to you.
I open the door.

Scripture to carry in your heart today:

Knock, and the door will be opened for you (Lk 11:9).

WEEK 2, DAY 4

POUNDING ON THE DOOR

I didn't pay attention to the knock.
Later I would remember
it didn't sound like an ordinary knock.
More like a fist pounding.
—SUE MONK KIDD

ANYONE WHO BANGS their fists on the door obviously hopes to get the attention of whoever is on the other side. What incites this type of behavior? The motivation usually centers around highly charged emotions, including a venting of frustration or anger. Pounding also happens due to fear, impatience, self-willed desire, a deep conviction of what is needed, or simply an urgent need for a response.

Pounding on the door provides a metaphorical way of describing an intense longing to make contact. Making a lot of noise implies, "I really need to connect with you, *now*!" This exaggerated action connotes the passionate relationship some feel toward the divine. Sufi poet Hafiz goes to the extreme in his visceral, ardent knocking on the Holy One's door:

> At night if I feel a divine loneliness
> I tear the doors off Love's mansion
> And wrestle God onto the floor.

Oh, to want God that much!

In Ann Weems' *Psalms of Lament* each prayer bears the excruciating screams of a mother's heart as she struggles to come to terms with her young son's homicide. Weems frequently pounds on God's door as she wails her anguish:

Open the door, O God!
Burst in and seize me
from the hell
of remembering!

Spirituality and religion can be "too nice." There are those who deem a strong emotional response to God inappropriate or unsuitable. There's nothing wrong with expressing unabashed passion or flailing highly charged outrage about unspeakable suffering upon the divine door and demanding to be heard. No more so than expressing a demure "please help me" or making a gentle tap of request. When we relate to the divine, we do so with our whole being. No part of our self ought to be left out.

Pounding is better than pretending things are all right. Trying to beat down the door allows a way to give voice to strong issues. It releases what keeps the soul tethered. However, this pounding cannot go on forever. Nursing bitterness over a loved one's death, perpetually blaming God for a wounded childhood or for the disappointments and struggles of one's life, these indicate that the pounding has to stop. The time comes to desist from beating on the door and begin redirecting one's energy toward eventual reconciliation and acceptance.

Whatever the reason for pounding on the door, one hopefully arrives at a place of resolution. No matter how deep and strong the pain in her psalms, Ann Weems ends each one with a verse similar to the Hebrew psalms that cry out with pain and struggle. Like these ancient prayers, once the desolate mother screams and pounds out her heartache and helplessness, she reluctantly but faithfully gives herself over to hope:

O God, I will continue
to ask, to seek, to knock
for you are the door of hope....
And the door will be
opened to me,
and I will live
in your blessing....

Maybe you are pounding on God's door today, or pounding on someone else's, and needing them to open their heart to you. Perhaps you are hammering on the door of your own heart, trying your utmost to get yourself to hear and accept what needs to be tended. Pray today for courage to be totally honest and for patience to wait for the door to be opened.

REFLECT ON THE FOLLOWING:

Is any part of your relationship with the Holy One in need of resolution?

MEDITATION

If strong emotions circle your heart and you sense a need to pound on God's door, speak these things to the Holy One. Do not be afraid to make yourself heard. End your reflection by voicing whatever hope you can rally. If you sense that *you* are the door being pounded on, listen for what demands to be heard. One way to do this is by taking pen in hand, asking the question, "What am I to hear?" and then writing for several minutes without stopping. Sit with what you've written and ask for guidance in how to respond to what came forth.

If your interior tenor is that of a quiet place with no need to beat on the door, sit in repose. Bask in the calm presence of the Holy One. Enjoy the silent communion.

PRAYER

Compassionate One,
tuck me into the sleeve of your love.
No matter what I express or cry out,
reassure me of your kindness and acceptance.
I believe in your endless offering of love.
Grant me the merciful grace to find hope
in the midst of what cries out to be heard.
I open the door to my heart to you.
I open the door.

When I cry aloud, be gracious to me and answer me! (Ps 27:7).

WEEK 2, DAY 5

TRUTH KNOCKS ON THE DOOR

The truth knocks on the door and you say,
"Go away. I'm looking for the truth"
and so it goes away. Puzzling.
—ROBERT PIRSIG

HOW DO I RESPOND when truth knocks on the door? My reaction depends on what truth is bringing me. Of course, I readily embrace truth that affirms the best part of who I am. If this type of truth comes, I eagerly respond: "Bring it on! I want to know!" But let truth sally up to the door with some incriminating evidence showing me an unwanted part of myself, then I'm hesitant, stand-offish, and reluctant to extend a welcome.

When truth frees us from our boxed-in notions of who we think we are, it's not uncommon for a certain amount of insecurity and fear to initially accompany truth's visitation. Only after this reality is welcomed and accepted does peace follow. Not long ago, I was culling my old journals and found something I wrote almost thirty years ago: "These words keep pounding on my mind's door this morning: tenacious, independent, strong-willed, dominant, head-strong, tough, determined. . . . Wow, yes, my strengths are also my weaknesses. . . ." I smiled, rather than grimaced, when I read that entry because I immediately felt gratitude for knowing these qualities about myself. Some would consider these characteristics to be helpful. They can be. At other times, these traits become my limitations. Being too tenacious or independent led me to hurt others and held me back from being a kind and forgiving person. Because of discovering and accepting this dimension, my limitations influence my thoughts and actions less than they did before truth knocked on my door. Recognition of my weaknesses has also helped me be softer in judgment of others' limitations, more merciful and understanding.

Ann O'Shaughnessy acknowledges the gift of truth, whether it is something desired or resisted, and recognizes it as an opportunity for expanding inner freedom:

> But what I keep discovering is that truth coupled with love and grace has a magical quality—creating doors where there were only walls and providing light on a path once hidden. A light so bright I can see it even as I drift from the known—untethered and a little afraid—into the unknown.

We are not alone in our reluctance to see what truth brings us. Numerous scriptural personages also drew back, hesitated, and questioned if the untethering was what they wanted. Mary of Nazareth questioned the message of her pregnancy and its consequences. Moses tried to throw off the call to lead his people through the wilderness. The rich person turned his back on truth when Jesus offered him what would truly change his life. Peter ignored the limitations of his boastfulness and pride. The Samaritan woman resisted the truth of her inherent goodness when Jesus invited her to accept it.

Like Ann O'Shaughnessy, I believe that when truth comes "with love and grace," we can find the courage to let it transform us. Here is a poem that arose from my depths at a time when love and grace were present for me:

> Truth
> Go ahead, look at me, through me,
> for you see what I hide from myself
> and the rest of the world.
> Go ahead, take those clear eyes
> and pierce the falseness with your reality.
> Draw open the thick door of my pretensions,
> my less than perfect self.
> My heart shivers under your penetrating gaze.

Only because your wisdom is stronger
than my dread, do I accept (hesitantly)
what you bring to my freshly opened door.

—JOYCE RUPP

Spend some time with truth today and notice your response when you recognize its message.

REFLECT ON THE FOLLOWING:

How has truth come knocking on your door? How has it affected your growth?

MEDITATION

Imagine you are sitting by a lake so clear you can see to the bottom of it. Look into your heart and find this same transparency. Gaze far inside. What do you see that you appreciate and treasure? What do you notice that you would rather not have? Sense divine love stirring through this lake of your deep self. Become aware of how your integrity shines as divine love moves the waters of your soul. Welcome the truth of your inherent goodness and be at peace with the gift of divinity stirring within you.

PRAYER

Loving Truth-Bringer,
there is always more for me to learn.
Your love and grace help me shed my falsity.
Enable me to welcome the truth of who I am.
Free me from the masks I choose to wear.
Reveal more of what has been unknown to me.
Clear away what keeps me from being transparent.
I open the door to my heart to you.
I open the door.

Jesus said, "You will know the truth, and the truth will make you free" (Jn 8:32).

WEEK 2, DAY 6

SLIPPING MESSAGES UNDER THE DOOR

Something inside me
Constantly bleeds towards god.
That's why I keep writing,
Slipping messages under the door.
—DOROTHY WALTERS

DOROTHY WALTERS TITLES the above poem "Why." So, why *does* she slip messages under the door? Has God seemingly not answered the door? Has the poet knocked and not received what she hoped for, or is she in one of those dark episodes of the soul when knocking seems fruitless?

What about the reverse situation? Could it be that the Holy One faithfully slips messages under our door when we fail to be aware of the divine knock? I have experienced both sides of this situation. I can be *the unaware one*, needing those divine raps at the entrance of my heart. And I, too, have had occasion to slip messages under the Holy One's door. Although I am truly convinced of God's unconditional love and fidelity, murky questions about the horrific violence inflicted by humanity and other unsettling issues go unresolved.

The German poet Rainer Maria Rilke expressed sentiments similar to those of Dorothy Walters when he, too, experienced a seeming lack of connection:

> You, God, who live next door—
> If at times, through the long night, I trouble you
> with my urgent knocking—
> this is why: I hear you breathe so seldom.

Even Walters's decision to not capitalize the "g" for God tells of what might be going on inside. There's a sense of distance indicated by the small "g." Perhaps the Holy One seems unavailable so she refuses to give the big "G" due acknowledgement. Whatever the reason, Walters has obviously not lost her desire to commune with this faithful presence. She is not about to give up her attempts to do so.

Those four brief lines composing the poem contain a remarkable amount of information and inspiration regarding the author's faith:

SOMETHING INSIDE ME . . .

Scholars, philosophers, contemplatives, and poets have attempted to define this "something" wedded to the soul, where the longing for the Great Mystery never dies. No words adequately describe this core of the authentic self, the gestating place where hunger for the Holy One rarely is fully satiated.

CONSTANTLY BLEEDS TOWARDS GOD . . .

Why the word "bleeds" when the author could have used "moves" instead? Blood, the life-giving element of the physical body, flows toward the heart center and back out of it. Walters indicates that "something" in her moves similarly toward God, her living center and focus of desire. Bleeding also suggests the possibility of a hurt or a wound. Is this the soreness of the soul, oozing toward the divine, longing for a bond that all too often seems to slip through the cry of one's longing?

"Constantly" tells us the poet has been at this for quite a while. I recall meeting a woman who lost all sense of divine presence. She told me she had experienced God as remote and unavailable for over thirty years. "That's a terrifically long, dark night of the soul," I exclaimed. She responded, "I have never given up praying. I've continued each day to be faithful to meditation and other spiritual practices."

SLIPPING MESSAGES UNDER THE DOOR . . .

Despite the estrangement, Walters does not cease trying to communicate with God. Her words encourage all who experience a distance, for whatever reason, between themselves and the divine. She reminds us that even if we do not sense God's nearness or experience a response to our knock on the door, faith carries us along, keeping us patient and steadfast. She prompts us to not give up.

We can do as this poet indicates: when God seems remote, continue to believe and trust that the divine is still accessible. We do not stop praying even though we have seemingly lost touch. We keep slipping messages under the door even when our sense of God's nearness snores away in us.

REFLECT ON THE FOLLOWING:

If you could slip a message to God under the door today, what would it be? What message might God slip under your door?

MEDITATION

Feel the pulse of your heartbeat, either on the inside of your wrist or by the carotid artery in your neck. Picture the blood in your body moving into the heart and out of the heart. Imagine God's love like the blood in your body, flowing into your heart and out, circulating through your life. Sit quietly and receive this movement of Eternal Presence filling your being with the spiritually life-giving essence of love. Renew your desire to be at one with this beloved Being.

PRAYER

Eternal Presence,
you are as intertwined with me
as blood is to my beating heart.
When I do not feel your nearness,
deepen my confidence in your love.
Restore any part of my wounded self
that hesitates to communicate with you.
I open the door of my heart to you.
I open the door.

SCRIPTURE TO CARRY IN YOUR HEART TODAY:

For God alone my soul waits in silence (Ps 62:1).

WEEK 2, DAY 7

REVIEW AND REST

THIS IS YOUR day to gather what has taken place for you during the past week of using this book. It is also meant to be a day of rest for you. Let this reflection and integration time be a gentle pause in your week. (You might choose to read the Introduction to the next week's prayer in the evening of this day or wait and begin fresh the next day, reading it at that time.)

BEGIN

"A Prayer for Openness" (page 13).

Review

Look back over the week. If you wrote in your journal, review what you've written. If you did not write, sit quietly for a few minutes and let your reflections from this week visit you. Then, respond in writing to the following:

1. The most helpful part of the past week's reflection and prayer was . . .
2. The most challenging part of the past week's reflection and prayer was . . .
3. I want to remember . . .
4. I hope that . . .
5. I wonder . . .

Complete your reflection with a one- or two-line summary of your experience from the week. An alternative to writing might be to summarize the week by drawing, sculpting, creating music, dancing, or using some other form of alternative expression to gather and integrate the week's experience into your present situation.

Another alternative to writing would be to summarize each week by drawing a door. Place words, phrases, drawings, or other symbols on the door to depict what happened within the week to draw you into further growth. (Instead of drawing a door, you could post these words, etc., on a real door in your home.)

Conclude

Close with one of the prayers from the week and/or by sitting quietly for a few minutes of gratitude.

Opening the Door

INTRODUCTION

Hurry! Hurry! Open every door says my heart.
—MARY OLIVER

WHEN I WAS a young child, the door to my inner self opened easily. The countryside invited contemplation and I readily responded. Of course, I had no idea what contemplation meant, but I spent a lot of time on the farm looking and listening, discovering and enjoying. Wondrous things claimed my heart. They spoke to me with their silent language of mystery and hope. Only in looking back do I see how simply and eagerly I opened the door, walking back and forth between the two worlds of my inner and outer self.

Gradually I moved away from the door to my inner world, closing the entrance to my transparent self as I accepted cultural and family messages focused on my external world. Several experiences in my twenties enabled me to begin reopening the door. First, I was introduced to meditation. With this fresh endeavor, I moved the door ajar cautiously and took a peek inside. About the same time, I began teaching young children. Their clear authenticity reminded me each day how firmly I had shut the door to my deeper self.

A few years after this, one of my younger brothers drowned. Rabindranath Tagore's words describe my response to that tragedy: "Within me there is a great disturbance/that has broken down all bars and doors." My brother's death sprang the hinges off the door. The ensuing grief after this death pushed me to take regular treks to the woods where I sought deliberate solitude. For the first time I kept a daily journal (which I have continued to do ever since). Each time I wrote in my notebook, I stepped further inside.

My time of solitude did exactly what Sufi scholar and teacher Neil Douglas-Klotz notes: "You thought you were going in one direction and toward a specific goal, but a mysterious doorway has appeared that seems to lead in a new direction." My brother's death led me to inner places I never dreamed I would go. One direction it aimed me was toward the constancy of divine presence. When my brother's death forced open the door, I stepped into grief and found the compassionate, all-embracing Holy One dwelling within me. I also discovered an inner resiliency I did not know I had, along with an ability to reach beyond self-pity toward a determined hope.

In one of David Whyte's talks, this gifted poet suggests that doors both "frighten and invite." While the thought of going within may be enticing, the actual process can feel much like that in Margaret Atwood's poem, "The Door."

> The door swings open,
> you look in.
> It's dark in there,
> most likely spiders;
> nothing you want.
> You feel scared.
> The door swings closed.

Having fear is understandable. Much depends on what we think is on the other side. Numerous persons, including ordained clergy, have disclosed their fears about this to me. Some doubt their inner worth. Others question whether they want or are able to accept the changes bound to come if they unlock the door to their true selves.

When my mother was introduced to certain topics and books, she would protest, "Oh, that's too deep for me." This tendency to steer clear from what might happen when we open to the authentic self has been observed by Jungian analyst Clarissa Pinkola Estés: "Women strengthen this barrier or door when they engage in a form of negative self-encouragement which warns them not to think or dive too deeply, for 'you may get more than you bargained for.'"

Our willingness to go within rests on courage to move beyond trepidation, faith to believe in our inner bountifulness, and hope that what we find will be a source of further growth. Having a skilled spiritual guide or an understanding friend reassures and supports us as we open the door. The best encouragement of all is the actual experience of gaining insight into who we truly are, of discovering a gem of authenticity that liberates and brings us peace.

Thomas Merton offers strengthening words of confidence about the inward journey:

> The Christ we seek is within us, in our inmost self, is our inmost self, and yet infinitely transcends ourselves. This is the very root of our being. Therefore, what we are called to do is to live as habitually and constantly as possible with great simplicity on this level of love which proceeds from the depths of our own being where Christ reigns and loves. This is a dimension of love which no one can take away unless we close the door ourselves and no one can bring it in unless we open the door to Christ, opening our hearts to Christ dwelling there.

Whether we open the door deliberately through spiritual practices and the aid of trusted companions or have the door thrust aside for us by unwanted or unexpected experiences, our deeper self awaits our entrance. The divine presence within this realm continually urges us inward. There is much to be discovered when we bravely wend our way there. Each opening of the door makes it worth the effort. We may not believe this initially, but with time we see and accept gratefully the wisdom our journey contains.

This week I invite you to stand before the door of your heart and open it. Remember Revelation 3:21. The Holy One stands at the door you are to open. Do not be afraid. Love in the fullest form accompanies you. Take a deep breath. Unlock the door. Reach slowly for the handle and swing wide the door of your heart.

WEEK 3, DAY 1

UNLOCKING THE DOOR

Within you lies all the courage you need. . . .
Solitude opens all the closed doors,
even those nailed shut.
—NANCY WOOD

A BEAUTIFUL "DANCE of Universal Peace" based on a thirteenth-century Sufi teaching advises those who seek love to sweep out the chambers of their heart, to make it ready so the Holy One can enter. As the words are sung, the dancers make an extensive sweeping movement of the arms outward from the heart, like the opening of a wide door. This movement follows with a generous gesture of gathering love into one's heart.

This dance presumes an opened heart in order to sweep out whatever keeps the divine guest from being received. Unfortunately, the heart's door is sometimes locked to the point of being double-bolted, padlocked, or even nailed shut depending on the severity of what caused the protected door to be firmly secured. The list of causes for locking the inner door is endless. Many things knowingly or unknowingly bar the door. Everything from bitter disappointment, emotional woundedness, and frenzied workaholism, to perfectionism, stubborn opinions, poor self-image, and fears aplenty. Some persons deliberately lock the door and others do so gradually by behaviors and attitudes developed over extended time. For those who are deeply wounded, it may take years to unlock the door.

In the gospel of Luke, Zechariah closes the door of his heart by refusing to believe his prayers have been answered. The angel tells Zechariah his aging wife will bear a son, but he rejects the amazing news. Zechariah then becomes mute until the birth of his son, John the Baptist, at which time his "mouth [is] opened." This story symbolizes how the inner door locks when we close the mind or heart to mystery (Lk 1:5–21, 57–80).

Whatever the reason for locking the door, eventually the door must be opened in order to learn and accept what brings continued growth. No matter how doubtful, apprehensive, or powerless we feel, we ought never give up hope of opening what is closed in us. The padlock on the door may have an impossible combination, but the Holy One can open even the most heavily defended door. As the English mystic Caryll Houselander puts it:

> It is for me that God awaits,
> with open hands,
> a beggar at the locked gates
> of my soul.

John's gospel assures us of this in the resurrection stories. He describes the frightened disciples huddled together after Christ's death, hiding in a place where "the doors of the house were locked." The secured door proved no problem for the Risen Christ. Twice he comes through doors locked out of fear. He entered "although the doors were locked, and stood in their midst and said, 'Peace be with you.'" A week later the disciples were once more in the house. Again, "although the doors were shut, Jesus comes, stands among them, saying, 'Peace be with you'" (Jn 20:19–26).

Love entered the room and freed the disciples' inner barriers. No matter how fortified or unyielding the door is, the divine comes to bring freedom and peace. This compassionate presence urges us to be less anxious, less defensive, less hostile, less self-deprecating or aggrandizing, less glued to protective postures and set ways of thinking.

Nancy Wood insists we have the courage to unlock doors, even those nailed shut. This noted poet and photographer advocates solitude as a way to do the unlocking. Why solitude? In the words of Henri Nouwen, "It is in solitude that inner freedom can grow. . . . In solitude we can slowly unmask the illusion of our possessiveness and discover in the center of our own self that we are not what we can conquer, but what is given to us." When we place ourselves in grace-filled solitude, we find space to hear the Holy One urging us to open the door.

Unlock the door today and breathe a sigh of relief.

REFLECT ON THE FOLLOWING:

Have I locked a door that keeps me from expanding my relationship with God, self, or others?

MEDITATION

Sit quietly. Enter into stillness. Picture Christ coming through the locked doors of the house where the disciples are hiding. Hear him say, "Peace be with you." Imagine the powerful release of apprehension that gradually took place in their hearts. Now, focus on a part of yourself that has a locked door or is wary of some aspect of growth. Imagine these words addressed to you: "Peace, peace to your heart." The words are repeated until peace settles within you. Let the locked door gradually open. Be at peace.

PRAYER

Risen Christ,
you came through the locked doors
of the fearful disciples' house.
Come through the locked doors
of my inner dwelling place.
Bring your enveloping peace
to where I am most in need of it.
I open the door of my heart to you.
I open the door.

SCRIPTURE TO CARRY IN YOUR HEART TODAY:

Peace be with you (Jn 20:26).

Week 3, Day 2

Oiling the Hinges

Take the time to pray—
it is the sweet oil that eases the hinge into the garden
so the doorway can swing open easily.
You can always go there.
—Lynn Park

I NEVER PAY attention to the hinge on a door until it starts to squeak, or worse, when it won't close because it's damaged, rusty, or just plain dried out due to a lack of lubrication. Some doors don't have hinges, but they still need to be oiled. There's a dilapidated sliding screen door on my patio that moves well for about a month or so. Eventually, it stutters and stalls, refusing to budge no matter what names I call it or how hard I push. Then I remember the solution and get out the WD-40 oilcan. A little spray on the top and bottom of the screen door tracks and, bingo, it moves effortlessly.

The hinges on the door of the heart also require attention. We forget about them until our openness falters. We know it's time to oil the hinges when self-pity consumes us, when we consistently feel cranky about life or get stuck and unyielding in relationships. We know we are not being our best self when we think we can get by without allowing time for prayer or when we work so hard we give little time to anyone or anything else. Whenever we sense inner conflict or get into a pout, it's definitely time to oil the hinges.

Here are some basic oils that keep the hinges of our heart moving smoothly.

Prayer

We already know we need this oil. Quiet, reflective periods are essential in order to keep the hinges from getting rusty. Prayer of any form and duration assists the door's ability to open.

Trust

The door to our interior chamber will not release adequately without trust. Our heart-door requires the oil of confidence in divine guidance and assurance in our ability to travel to the deeper places.

Love

Love that is large, not small, that's the kind of oil a heart-door uses. The contents of this lubrication include ample amounts of generosity, other-centeredness, and a nonjudgmental attitude toward self and others. With this indispensable oil, we can do what Dawna Markova advises:

> Let us swing wide all the doors and windows
> of our hearts on their rusty hinges
> so we may learn how to open in love.

Patience

This oil makes it possible to not give up trying to keep the door ajar. Patience prevents our inner door from getting stuck in discouraging thoughts and feelings.

Forgiveness

Just about the time we set this oilcan in the closet, a hostile person or a memory of a past hurt comes along and bluntly reminds us to keep forgiveness near at hand. A large amount of this oil may have to be applied before some doors swing freely.

Creativity

The necessity for this oil might surprise you. Its purpose is to allow our innate gifts to birth into life, thus easing the door's opening movement so we can express our genuine self.

Faithfulness

The hinges of the heart's door expect a daily lubrication of this oil. Faithfulness assures our daily efforts' continuance, even though we might think *nothing is happening* when we attempt to open the door.

Surrender

Sometimes it is best to stop pushing when our heart-door is unyielding and admit we need assistance to release it. Get the oilcan of surrender out. Go to God and others. Ask for help.

Leisure

This oil renews our energy. Leisure clears our mind and heart. It restores our receptivity toward what happens when we open the door.

Did I miss any oil for the hinges? You might have a few more in mind. Check the hinges of your heart-door regularly. Be sure they are in good working condition so you move easily, back and forth, between the inner and outer realms of your life.

REFLECT ON THE FOLLOWING:

What kind of oil do the hinges on your heart-door currently need?

MEDITATION

Find a door in your home that has hinges. Take a look at the door. Open and close it. Notice what a gift a hinge is to that door. Stand quietly by the hinges and listen to your deeper self for a few minutes. Pay close attention to how you are loving, or not loving, yourself and others. Notice any place where you feel stuck or unable to grow. You may hear a squeak or two in your heart. Is it time for some oil? If so, decide what kind of oil you need and when you will apply it. On the other hand, you may hear a silent sigh of peace. If so, put the oilcan away and be grateful.

Trusted Companion,
at certain times the door to my heart
squeaks with willful resistance.
It also gets rusty from lack of use,
refuses to budge and won't loosen.
Come with your oilcan of grace-filled love.
Release what keeps me from being true to you.
I open the door of my heart to you.
I open the door.

SCRIPTURE TO CARRY IN YOUR HEART TODAY:
You anoint my head with oil; my cup overflows (Ps 23:5).

WEEK 3, DAY 3

THE OPENER

I am the gate. . . .
The gatekeeper opens the gate. . . .
—JOHN 10:9, 3

THE ABOVE TWO verses from John's gospel point to a spiritual paradox. Jesus teaches that he is both the *door* and the *opener* of the door. This metaphor of the divine door-opener is a tenet of the Christian tradition and also of other religious faiths. In the Muslim faith, the Sufis (the mystical branch of Islam) chant "dhikr" or "zikr," using one of their "ninety-nine most beautiful names" for Allah in which they repeat the divine name for lengthy periods of prayer. One of my favorite descriptions among the list of beautiful names is that of "Al-Fattah," the opener.

[Al-Fattah] is the Opener and the Solver, the Easer of all that is locked, tied and hardened. There are things that are closed to one. There are states and problems that are tied in a knot. These are hardened things that one cannot see through and pass through. Some are material things: professions, jobs, gains, possessions, places, friends that are unavailable to one. There are also hearts tied in a knot with sadness, minds tied up in doubts or questions they are unable to answer.

Allah al-Fattah opens them all. There is nothing unavailable to the beloved servant of Allah, for whom al-Fattah opens all gates. No force can keep those doors locked. But if Allah does not open the doors . . . , no force can make those doors open. . . .

The Book of Revelation attributes the characteristic of the door-opener to Jesus and presents him as saying, "Look, I have set before you an open door, which no one is able to shut" (Rv 3:8). One has only to read through the Christian scriptures to see how Jesus obviously exemplifies an opener. He clears the eyes of the blind: "Then he touched their eyes . . . and their eyes were opened" (Mt 9:29–30). He opens the ears of the deaf: "He said to him, 'Ephphatha,' that is, 'Be opened.' And immediately [the deaf man's] ears were opened" (Mk 7:34–35). He frees the hearts of seekers: "The Lord opened [Lydia's] heart to listen eagerly to what was said by Paul" (Acts 16:14). He expands the minds of those who are confused: "Were not our hearts burning within us while he was talking to us on the road, while he was opening the scriptures to us?" (Lk 24:32).

While Jesus opened physical eyes and ears, his deeper message centered on an interior releasing that led people to the freedom of becoming their truest selves. Opening the heart is as much a miracle as a physical healing. I look back on my own life and am amazed at how the Holy One assisted me to open the door to qualities I did not know I had, to attitudinal changes, to a clearance in my mind and heart that brought about healing and serenity.

When the door to our deeper self opens, either through our desire to grow or through unexpected and unwanted events, we can be tricked by the ego into thinking we do this growing by our selves. When this happens we easily succumb to the anxiousness of trying to push and control our spiritual growth. We forget that we do not open the door by our efforts alone. When we acknowledge our desire to grow and turn our heart toward the Opener, we discover that God's "power at work within us is able to accomplish abundantly far more than all we can ask or imagine" (Eph 3:20).

With divine assistance, we disarm the door. We let go of the armor of the heart. When we do so, the miracle of our spiritual growth occurs. We begin to see how we are to live and act. We hear the summons of our inner Companion and enter the path to our authentic self. We allow this guidance to daily shape our vision by leading us from a narrow, self-oriented blindness to spacious sight, from crippling attitudes to loving actions, from the shadows of ignorance to a wisdom that truly sets us free.

As you move through this day, take the Opener with you. If there is hesitation in your heart, turn to the Holy One for assistance in releasing the goodness within yourself. The Opener does not force anyone. Each is free to enter and explore the landscape of the soul in the context of one's own journey. Be at peace with what you can or cannot do at this time.

REFLECT ON THE FOLLOWING:

In what particular aspect of your life do you most need divine assistance to open the door to your authentic self? What keeps you from receiving this assistance?

MEDITATION

Sit quietly, paying particular attention to your breath . . . coming in . . . going out. . . . When you have stilled your body, mind, and spirit, visualize the Opener coming to you and holding out a hand to you. When you take it, you are led to a door. This is the one that needs opening in your life. Stand before that door. Sense the power of love in the Opener's heart moving into yours. Receive the strength of this love. Together, the two of you open the door to your inner chamber and enter the hallowed space. Remain there for as long as you wish. Bring the assuredness of divine love with you as you leave your heart-space and close your meditation. Take the gift of this transforming presence with you into the day.

PRAYER

> Ever-Present Opener,
> you offer me your love and strength.
> You can help me open any door.
> Lead me to where my truest self dwells.
> I reach out to receive the freedom and courage
> you extend to me at this very moment.
> Transform my life into one that reflects your love.
> I open the door of my heart to you.
> I open the door.

SCRIPTURE TO CARRY IN YOUR HEART TODAY:

> I can do all things through God who strengthens me (Phil 4:13).

WEEK 3, DAY 4

OPENING TO ONENESS

Not knowing when the dawn will come
I open every door.
—EMILY DICKINSON

OPENING THE DOOR to the inner self is reminiscent of a new day's dawning. Morning serves as a sentinel of wakefulness. With daybreak comes the movement out of sleep. Night closes the door to its thick layers of obscurity, and dawn signals the first breath of light. The inner openings of our heart experience a similar awakening. Emily Dickinson wisely observed that we do not know for sure when the light of clarity and insight comes. Thus, we live with alert readiness to let go of the night of our unknowing and receive whatever encourages greater oneness with our true self and the Great Love who dwells there.

Reflecting on the topic of spiritual growth, Canadian author Judith Campbell, writes:

> When we don't open ourselves to the spiritual opportunities that exist for us, it is like living our lives within only one windowless room of a house, never having explored the rest of the house or gone outside to see what awaits us there. And within this one room, we focus only on our physical being—on our basic needs that keep us alive and fuel an egocentric way of being. When we share this room with like-minded people, we remain stuck within this physical place, unable to see the light of day that calls to us from the other side of the door.

When we open the door of our heart to what beckons us inward, we become adventurers of the unknown territory of our being. We do not stay with what is identified and secure. We move outside the "one windowless room" and explore what lies beyond. We do what author Judy Cannato advocates: ". . . we reject any temptation that keeps us from self-communion, from tending to the Holy One who dwells within." Like the dawn bringing illumination to the day, the journey to our authentic self holds countless findings waiting to enlighten us. The doors we open ultimately lead to the genuine nucleus of our self, affording us the opportunity to shed the falseness to which we once tightly clung.

The more we enter our core reality, the more our true self becomes available to us. When we seek to unite with our inherent goodness (our God-ness), we often encounter obstacles to love that try to thwart our pursuit. We find a lot of inner cobwebs hiding neglected virtues. In addition, we usually uncover dusty corners of useless debris discarded from who we thought we were. Such is the adventure and challenge of uniting more intimately with what is integral to our authenticity. Some opened doors lead to shedding and some lead to embracing. All the opened places of the heart eventually move us into oneness with radiant Love.

In *Christian Meditation: Experiencing the Presence of God,* James Finley offers encouraging words about this process:

> The beloved says from the other side of the door, "Open the door and come in, so we can experience just how one we might become." You stand outside the door, reading one more book about how to open the door. You note in your journal one more thought about what it might be like to walk through the door. And all the while the longings of your heart remain unconsummated. And so let today be the day you open the door of your heart to God, whose heart, from all eternity, is open to you. . . . God has left the door unlocked and even slightly ajar. God is waiting for you to open it and come walking through to experience that oneness with God that is the fullness of life itself.

Each day the Dawn-Bringer calls to us: "Open the door. Explore what you believe and know. Investigate what you do not believe and do not know. Seek my dawning light within the fragments of your daily happenings. Search within yourself for paths that lead to love. Lift the shades off the windows of your shadowy heart-room. Welcome each secret that shows its face to you. Venture into illuminating self-acceptance so more of my radiant beauty shines forth from you."

REFLECT ON THE FOLLOWING:

What action will you choose today to help you open the door to oneness?

MEDITATION

Pause in silence to allow stillness, courage, and confidence to awaken in your being. Visualize the ending of night with its obscure layers of darkness. Picture colorful rays of early sunshine rising on an eastern horizon. Notice how the dawn brings the ability to see things clearly. Turn your mind and heart toward the Holy One. Pray for clarity of mind and heart. Cherish the inner radiance of the Dawn-Bringer's presence. Enter into the oneness of love that is offered to you. Accept this gift with gratitude as you go forth from your meditation.

Great Awakener,
the doors to spiritual transformation
and lasting oneness are here with you.
For every door that has opened, thank you.
I move with confidence and hope
toward doors yet to disclose the unknown.
Each day I will seek your dawning light.
I open the door of my heart to you.
I open the door.

SCRIPTURE TO CARRY IN YOUR HEART TODAY:
Abide in me as I abide in you (Jn 15:4).

WEEK 3, DAY 5

SOME DOORS OPEN SLOWLY

My heart is too uncertain for a cosmic event.
Its doors open one at a time, and slowly.
—JOY COWLEY

IN OUR EXTERNAL world we are used to opening doors and passing through quickly. In our inner world, the movement is ordinarily much slower. At times, we hesitate before the door. We may not be able to find the key or are uncertain if this is the right door. We may question if we have enough time to spend inside. At other times, we are eager to get moving, to leap through the door and zoom into the new truth. In this instance, as soon as we realize a fresh dimension of spiritual growth, or see something about us that needs freeing, we rush in and work hard at being changed as quickly as possible.

Trying to induce our inner growth only creates anxiety and self-doubt. Spiritual transformation requires time in the same way that physical gestation does. We do not grow ourselves in a day anymore than a child in the womb develops in less than an allotted period of maturation. Macrina Wiederkehr writes about the wisdom of growing unhurriedly and notes that "the disciple in each of us is awakened slowly."

Opening the door to our inmost self entails ample amounts of patience. No matter how much control and effort we invest in growing, we cannot force our inner maturity. In spite of our willingness and hurrying, the doors open when they are ready. Paula D'Arcy puts it this way in her book, *Sacred Thresholds:*

> "Don't push the river," says my friend Richard Rohr. Don't get ahead of your soul. The goal isn't to get somewhere. The goal isn't about forcing something to happen. The goal is to be in harmony with the gifts that are already given. The goal is to fall in love with your life.

If we yank at and shove the door, demanding to immediately gain greater self-awareness and oneness with God, we will tend to obsessively focus on this effort and easily miss a good portion of our life where the Holy One already draws us closely into love.

Some tension will continually exist between giving ourselves to spiritual growth while living gratefully with what has already been given. But when we get too pushy about the inner journey, there's a tendency to fall into despondency and discouragement. When this happens, a gloomy self-doubt gradually overtakes the desire to open the door, causing us to forfeit our longing to grow. Gunilla Norris describes this inner movement in an accurate way.

> If we do not have immediate and recognizable
> progress we feel like quitting.
> Here is where many of us give up.
> We shut the door. We say,
> What's the use? I don't see anything different.

This is not adding up to anything.
I don't feel any better, and I'm not able to do this.

While inner growth cannot be forced or hurried, we give ourselves as fully as possible to the process. I recognized this in a letter that came from a woman named Pat who desperately wanted to move beyond grief over her mother's death. In her sorrow, Pat kept pressing on the door, hoping she would be freed from her endless sorrow. In her words, "I have been struggling terribly. I had gone through a couple of phases of praying a lot, begging for God's comfort—to no avail. Nobody seemed to understand my level of pain."

Several months later, when Pat finally stopped pushing and surrendered to the slow healing from her grief, she wrote to tell me that the door released with the discovery of an unexpected article. It led her to "hope and reserved excitement." Once she gave her grief time to gestate and move into a different reality, Pat discovered a deeper sense of her present relationship: "I thought God would be there the way I wanted God to be—but now I am better able to recognize God's touch. . . . I am hoping that, at some point, I will be able to understand the depths of God's love for me."

Remember today that doors open slowly. Pray to be patient.

Reflect on the following:

Are you hurrying any part of your growth? Is it keeping you from falling in love with your life?

Meditation

Close your eyes. Take a journey through your evolving relationship with God. Think of the ways you have grown since you were first introduced to this divine companion. Turn your heart in trust as you look toward what most longs to grow in your life now. Sit silently. On each in-breath, pray: "I place my trust in you." Continue with this breath-prayer until you come to a sense of peace.

Source of Transformation,
when I too eagerly hurry my growth
or try to hastily shove my way
into a deeper relationship with you,
soften my impatient determination.
Remind me of the time it takes
to gestate this growth in my soul.
I open the door of my heart to you.
I open the door.

SCRIPTURE TO CARRY IN YOUR HEART TODAY:
Wait . . . be strong, and let your heart take courage (Ps 27:14).

WEEK 3, DAY 6

WELCOMING THE UNWANTED

The open door to true peace with the self
is the door that opens on to belonging to the sum,
the whole, in thought and word and deed.
—LATIFA ZAYYAT

WHEN WE OPEN the door to the true self, we uncover more of the sum of who we are. Initially, this may lead to discomfort instead of peace, for not everything we find is what we want. But if we befriend what is within us and are willing to learn from it, serenity will ultimately reign at the center of our being.

When I was in my thirties I had a rude awakening. The more faithful I was to daily meditation and prayer, the more I came to see how self-centered

I could be. As I opened the door to my deeper self, out jumped the reality of an ego that wanted life to revolve around "me." This truth was enough to scare me off completely from journaling and prayer, but I kept on because the taste of truth was stronger than living with deception. By regular observation, I heard how loud the ego's voice was as it eagerly sought to let others know how "I" was doing, what "I" was thinking, where "I" was going, but failed to ask and listen to the experience of the other person. Gradually, I taught this part of "me" to behave, to be as interested in others as I was in myself. I grew in becoming a good listener. This painful awareness also helped me differentiate between what is self-centeredness and what is healthy self-love, to know and value my best self while not allowing the ego to continually announce its presence

Everyone has some ogres hidden in their heart. They show up at the strangest times, as they did in noted author Anne Lamott's life: "The door to the most primitive place inside me opened, where the betrayed child lives, terrified, wounded, murderous. On top of everything, I felt a deep, familiar self-loathing." These unwanted traits of ours throttle us with their unmanageable and mouthy insertion into daily life. If left unattended, they cripple spiritual development. If recognized, they can be dealt with and tamed.

The experience of discovering these traits naturally disheartens us, especially when we try to get rid of them and they keep having their way. The most helpful approach is to get to know these unwanted qualities as thoroughly as possible. (What we fail to know or refuse to acknowledge only gains power over us.) Welcoming these difficult traits keeps them within the boundaries of our attention and does not allow them to leap into action as readily. Some unwanted characteristics perpetuate their existence throughout life but, if corralled, they do not get to rule us. Other undesirable traits gradually cease after we acknowledge them, to the point where they rarely intrude on our life.

An encouraging message of the well-known Swiss psychologist C. G. Jung to accept ourselves as we are, brings with it both comfort and challenge. Jung suggests that just as Christ urges us to love our enemy, give alms to the beggar, and forgive the one who offends us, so we are called to approach our self in the same way. Jung proffers: "But what if I discover that the least of all . . . the poorest of all beggars, the most insolent of all offenders, yes, even the very enemy . . . that these live within me, that I myself stand in need of the alms of my own kindness, that I am to myself the enemy who is to be loved, what then?"

Such a powerful question. Such a demanding requirement—that we learn to love the totality of who we are. Can we come near to ourselves with the same love Christ had when he drew near to those with qualities deemed unacceptable? When Buddhist nun Pema Chödrön writes about making peace with these characteristics we tend to reject, she reminds her readers: "No one else knows what it takes for another person to open the door. For some people, speaking out is opening the door a little wider; for other people, being still is opening the door a little wider." As we get to know our whole self, we know what part of us especially needs our understanding and care.

When we open the door to the unwanted parts of our self, we have the full support of our Great Love who knows every part of us, who believes in us and accepts the sum of who we are. I hope that this day encourages you to approach yourself in that same loving manner.

REFLECT ON THE FOLLOWING:
What unwanted part of yourself waits to be welcomed and tended?

MEDITATION
Think of a gospel scene where Jesus welcomes someone unacceptable. Put yourself in the scene. Envision yourself as the unacceptable one with the part of you that you do not like or want in yourself. Approach Jesus (or another form of the divine) and allow yourself to be embraced with loving kindness. Receive this unconditional love. Let it wrap around your entire self. Allow the unwanted aspect in yourself to speak to you. When you have heard what this part of you wants, talk to it about what you expect of it. Close the meditation by allowing yourself to sit serenely in the embrace of the Holy One.

PRAYER

Embracer of the Rejected,
teach me how to lovingly welcome
the parts of myself that I do not want.
Draw me to your heart of mercy
as I learn from what I tend to reject.
Help me to change what I can
and to accept the sum of who I am.
I open the door of my heart to you.
I open the door.

SCRIPTURE TO CARRY IN YOUR HEART TODAY:

Likewise the Spirit helps us in our weakness (Rom 8:26).

WEEK 3, DAY 7

REVIEW AND REST

THIS IS YOUR day to gather what has taken place for you during the past week of using this book. It is also meant to be a day of rest for you. Let this reflection and integration time be a gentle pause in your week. (You might choose to read the Introduction to the next week's prayer in the evening of this day or wait and begin fresh the next day, reading it at that time.)

BEGIN

"A Prayer for Openness" (page 13).

Review

Look back over the week. If you wrote in your journal, review what you've written. If you did not write, sit quietly for a few minutes and let your reflections from this week visit you. Then, respond in writing to the following:

1. The most helpful part of the past week's reflection and prayer was . . .
2. The most challenging part of the past week's reflection and prayer was . . .
3. I want to remember . . .
4. I hope that . . .
5. I wonder . . .

Complete your reflection with a one- or two-line summary of your experience from the week. An alternative to writing might be to summarize the week by drawing, sculpting, creating music, dancing, or using some other form of alternative expression to gather and integrate the week's experience into your present situation.

Another alternative to writing would be to summarize each week by drawing a door. Place words, phrases, drawings, or other symbols on the door to depict what happened within the week to draw you into further growth. (Instead of drawing a door, you could post these words, etc., on a real door in your home.)

Conclude

Close with one of the prayers from the week and/or by sitting quietly for a few minutes of gratitude.

STANDING ON THE THRESHOLD

INTRODUCTION

The breeze at dawn has secrets to tell you.
Don't go back to sleep. . . .
People are going back and forth across the doorsill
where the two worlds touch.
The door is round and open.
Don't go back to sleep.

—JALALUDDIN RUMI

IN THE FIRST moment of awakening from sleep, the two worlds of unconscious slumber and conscious alertness briefly touch. As we yawn and prepare to rise, we move from one sphere to the other. The unseen boundary between these two worlds is known as a *threshold*. Like the physical doorsills over which we cross, we also move across interior ones. Each step across the unseen doorsill allows entry into the mystery of our deeper self.

The threshold of our invisible self signifies a separation between inner and outer space such as spirit and body, between nonmaterial spheres like the known and the unknown self, between the hidden and the manifested areas of our life. The threshold can also be likened to a *thin veil*, a term ancient Celts used to indicate the numinous in-between that separates this world from that of the spiritual ancestors. Certain Celtic people with a special inner sight were said to communicate with the ancestors by crossing back and forth between this world and the ethereal one of spirit.

The metaphor of the threshold aptly describes a vital component of our spiritual journey. This symbolic line marks the division between who we are now and who we will become, between present awareness of the Holy One and how this relationship develops in the future. Angeles Arrien describes the worth of the threshold metaphor this way:

> Throughout history, images of thresholds and gates have served as symbolic passageways into new worlds. Imprinted on the human psyche, they herald the possibility of a new life, a new experience,

or a new identity. They offer an opportunity for communion between different worlds: the sacred and profane, the internal and external, the subjective and objective, the visible and invisible, waking and dreaming.

A physical threshold grants passage between two different external spaces, while a nonphysical threshold allows entrance and exit from our inner world. This invisible line of demarcation provides space and time to ponder and assess our spiritual direction. If we choose to cross over and enter our inner space, we move into a more comprehensive sense of self and further activation of our vast potential of goodness. This is why the term *threshold experience* indicates a significant turning point, one that urges us to look for further clarity regarding our essential beliefs, choices, and actions.

Spiritual transformation often comes at a price. There will be times when we find ourselves unsure, hesitant, doubting, and questioning which way to go with our life, wishing we were anywhere but on the threshold's teetering vagueness. We are rarely the same after experiencing the inner threshold.

Not all threshold experiences are huge. Some are brief but highly opportune for our growth. Something like a simple story or a line from a poem holds enough potential to cause us to suspend a firmly held truth and eventually change our focus. Some thresholds contain joyous transitions, like entering into a loving relationship or resolving an old family issue. Other thresholds bring discomfort and uneasiness. Sometimes these dark crossings include clinical depression and are extremely painful due to extended ambiguity and an intense sense of feeling lost and alone.

In *Jubilee Time,* Maria Harris reminds her readers that the "threshold is a place of the spirit, uniting the mundane with the mysterious, the commonplace with the awesome." She details how this call to move into unknown territory recurs in biblical themes, beginning with "the banishing of Adam and Eve from the mythical Eden, to the passage out of Egypt and on through the parting of the Sea of Reeds, to the final invitation to enter a new Jerusalem where death and mourning shall be no more. . . ." During this threshold time, Harris says, "we are being lured to open the doors of our hearts and the gates of our spirits."

Jan Richardson also sees spiritual significance in the threshold. In *Night Visions,* she writes:

The word threshold originally referred to the doorway leading to the place where the threshing of grain occurred. Beyond the entrance lay the place of separating the wheat from the chaff, of sorting and sifting, of beginning to cull that which would become bread. John the Baptist used this image as he spoke of how Jesus would come to clear the threshing floor and gather the wheat. John's words served as a vivid warning to the people to prepare, to consider whether they were ready to walk through the doorway toward the life to which Jesus would call them.

The gift of the threshold provides a way to cross over into a fuller life of spiritual depth and freedom. When we choose to traverse the invisible boundary of the known self and enter the unknown, we are saying: Yes, I want to grow, to become wiser, to be strengthened, to be less burdened by what weighs me down and keeps me from being my authentic self. I am willing to pay the price for this growth.

This week I invite you to open the door of your heart and stand on the threshold of your own particular path. I trust you will find what is essential for your growth.

WEEK 4, DAY 1

THE POWER OF THE THRESHOLD

The Resurrection is not a single event, but a loosening
of God's power and light into the earth and into history
that continues to alter all things, infusing them
with the grace and power of God's own holiness.
It is as though a door was opened, and what poured out
will never be stopped, and the door cannot be closed.
—MEGAN MCKENNA

THINK OF WHAT happens to a caterpillar when it enter
ing passageway of the chrysalis as it is being transformed int
Imagine a parched land with the threshold of an enormous th
brewing before rain sings itself into thirsty ground. Conside
special place of beauty to watch a sunrise. As you sit on the doorsill of
darkness and wait silently, light fills the horizon. Each of these situations
illustrates the threshold's value as a channel of change.

A threshold contains the power of transformation. In this place of
uncertainty and decision making, we are forced to slow down and take
stock of what's happening. This is where we yield to the necessary gestation that grows us into greater freedom. During this time we let go of old
ego ways we formerly relied upon to defend us from insecurity or facili-
tate resistance. All one's energy must be given to the process that readies
us for the next tentative step of development.

Threshold times cleanse us of false perceptions and wean us from
feeding on what no longer nurtures. These passageways serve as spiritual
wombs where the soul grows stronger wings in spite of doubts about
whether those wings can soar freely. Threshold experiences contain tremendous energy. They hold the power to unglue and shake us deeply, to
enfold us with a seemingly empty darkness that causes us to yearn for
relief. They can set an imprisoned spirit free, nurse a wounded heart back
to health, and bring peace to a desolate mind.

I believe in this power of transformation because of my own threshold experiences. One of these darkened periods took place when my father died suddenly of a heart attack. His death plunked me immediately
on a doorsill of grief where I stayed for over a year. Oh, how I yearned to
go back through the door to the past and undo his death. I wanted to go
to the last time I was with him, to say the things that never got said, to
hear his laugh, to hug him and say goodbye one more time. During this
threshold of immobility and sadness, I did not know what was gestating.
Only as depression lifted was I able to move beyond my immobilization
to renewed hope. Only then did I realize how compassion had grown in
me. Strengthened and purified by the threshold's energy, I could empa-
thize more fully with the pain of others who knew loss and let it sit inside
my heart.

Another threshold I stood on was also not of my choosing. A new director of the staff at my place of ministry developed an edge of hostility toward my work and related to me with animosity. After two years of this, we still could not resolve our conflicting differences. I regrettably left the work I enjoyed. The decision to quit pushed me onto a gloomy threshold. I despised being there. I wanted to leap off, kick the door to the past shut as fast as I could, and move toward the future. But I stayed in that gestating spot until I yielded to its power to ease my discouragement and anger.

I could not envision how this bleak in-between place could be a preparation for my future. Yet, as acceptance and forgiveness grew in my heart, I eventually walked through the doorway into renewed serenity and a more satisfying work, the kind I always wanted to do. I would never have moved beyond the door of my past work had it not been for being pushed onto the unwanted threshold and eventually finding an unforeseen opportunity.

The power of a threshold resounds in the story of the resurrection. From the hollow deadness of the tomb, Christ came forth transformed with unmistakable splendor. So in our threshold experiences, the Holy One's life-giving energy frees and gifts us with what enables us to express the beauty of our soul.

Reflect on the following:
What threshold experience changed your life significantly?

Meditation
Sit on a chair that is placed across a doorsill. Recall the formation of a caterpillar into a butterfly. First, see the caterpillar crawling along, munching leaves. Then, visualize this little creature creating the chrysalis in which it will hang. Imagine you are inside this quiet, dark space of metamorphosis. Let yourself sit quietly inside that threshold of change for as long as you can. You do not need to do anything but just "be there." After some quiet time, picture a brilliant monarch butterfly coming forth from the chrysalis. Join in the wonder and freedom of its first flight.

Close this reflection by turning your heart in trust toward the One who brings you fullness of life.

PRAYER

> Gestating Spirit,
> your gifts of transformation
> await me on every threshold.
> Your life-giving power raised Christ
> from the bleak tomb of darkness.
> Raise what has died in me.
> Refresh it with your touch of love.
> I open the door of my heart to you.
> I open the door.

SCRIPTURE TO CARRY IN YOUR HEART TODAY:
I came that they may have life, and have it abundantly (Jn 10:10).

WEEK 4, DAY 2

THE LIMINAL SPACE

*It's as if we were caught in a darkened vestibule
between an old way of being and a new. . . . The doors
of the past close behind us. The doors to the future
are still unopened. Too often we forget that only by
enduring our time in the liminal space between those
doors, waiting for an opening, can we eventually move
freely across a threshold into the future.*
—JANE R. PRÉTAT

THE "LIMEN" IS another way of describing the in-between space of a doorway. The term "liminality" indicates the uncomfortable ambiguity that develops when we are standing in the middle of a juncture of significant change. Liminality implies a disoriented vagueness in which we wander about searching for what seems out of reach. We lose a sense of clear identity, question what seems to be a dissolving relationship with our self and, perhaps, with our God. All of which leads us to review the values and beliefs that give our life meaning.

Liminal space is a twilight time when it is neither day nor night. Things cannot be seen clearly in the dusky grayness washing over our mind and heart. In *Journey of the Soul,* Doris Klein does not use the word "liminal," but she certainly describes its unsettling experience:

> When we face those times of uncertainty in our life, the scene is often blurry. Things we were so sure of suddenly make little sense. The answers we thought were clear now seem lost in a distant fog, and we wander aimlessly, unable to regain the focus we once believed we had. Our confusion is unsettling. Doubt, like vertigo, distorts our balance as we fearfully wander in a vast and empty inner wilderness. As we wrestle with the darkness, a rush of panic washes into our hearts, our breath becomes shallow and, with each question, the judgments seem to escalate.

Even the strongest of spirits feels the effect of liminality. Renowned meditation teacher Jack Kornfield tells of how he learned to be aware of his inner self, including the difficult parts, when he was studying in Thailand. Part of his meditation training was to go alone in the dark of night to be in the forest where he was sent to reflect on death. Kornfield said that:

> sitting in a dark forest with its tigers and snakes was easier than sitting with my inner demons. My insecurity, loneliness, shame, and boredom came up. All my frustrations and hurts, too. . . . Little by little I learned to face them with mindfulness, to make a clearing within the dark woods of my own heart.

It is not unusual to want to avoid the threshold. During liminality we may well be challenged to see our wounded and unwelcome side.

Who deliberately seeks this kind of discomfort? Who wants to know the hidden parts like those Kornfield describes? Yet, this discovery holds an essential gift for growth. The hidden hurts and the false stuff that have accumulated are acknowledged and let go. When this happens, the blessedness of our self has more room to reveal its transforming authenticity.

Being in liminal space is like swinging on a trapeze. Once the handle is released there is nothing to hold onto until the handle on the other side is caught. We are no more sure of what lies beyond the threshold than the trapeze artist flying into the open in-between space knows for sure she will catch the other handle. Liminality requires acceptance of mystery and a heart full of trust. The challenge is to give ourselves fully to the process of change while being unsure and unclear of how this liminal time will affect our future.

Doris Klein offers good advice:

> When these times of mystery seem endless and our souls become weary of the stretch to believe, our prayer must be a simple request—that we be reminded that we have not been abandoned in this place to wander forever alone . . . for it is often a silent flicker in our heart, the tiny voice within, that whispers wordlessly, "You are always loved. You are never alone."

Take heart today as you remember those whispered words.

REFLECT ON THE FOLLOWING:

What is unclear, unresolved, confusing, or perplexing about your spiritual journey?

MEDITATION

Once again, place your chair across the threshold of a doorway. Sit down and put your hands on your lap, palms facing up and opened. Breathe in divine love. Breathe out whatever keeps you from trusting this love with your entire life. Mentally place in your open hands whatever confusion, uncertainty, questions, or disorientation you have. Give these inner stirrings into the care of the Holy One. Unite with this love as fully as you can. Be at peace.

Mysterious One,
when I stand in liminality
you stand there with me.
You hold my doubts, questions,
darkness and disturbances
in the safe embrace of your love.
You will guide me to clarity and peace.
I open the door of my heart to you.
I open the door.

SCRIPTURE TO CARRY IN YOUR HEART TODAY:
O Most High, when I am afraid, I put my trust in you (Ps 56:2).

WEEK 4, DAY 3

THE NARROW DOOR

Enter through the narrow gate; for the gate is
wide and the road is easy that leads to destruction,
and there are many who take it. For the gate is
narrow and the road is hard that leads to life, and
there are few who find it.
—MATTHEW 7:13–14

SOME BIBLICAL TRANSLATIONS use "gate" and others use "door," but whenever I hear anyone preach on the above text, almost every person speaks about the narrow and wide aspects in relation to being saved or unsaved. Jesus uses neither of these two salvific words in this particular passage. What he does employ, in order to get people's full attention, is a hyperbolic or exaggerated form of speaking. He urges his listeners to deliberately choose to live with spiritual intention and purpose. As Jesus explains, this is no easy thing to do, not in a culture that tries its best to divert attention from the soul's oneness with its eternal source.

Wide gate and narrow gate. Destruction and life. Two opposing possibilities. What do these two doors represent? The wide gate does not symbolize a call to alienate ourselves from the world or to suffocate joy and satisfaction. Rather, the wide gate indicates an expanse so vast that anything and everything passes through it. There is no restraint, no focus, no discernment about what might be helpful and what might be harmful. Anything goes. No limits. In the wide door approach to life, little of what is experienced is weighed as to the consequences upon one's life and that of others, or of how it affects one's relationship with God.

In this particular teaching, going through the wide gate damages the soul's journey because it distracts from what engages the soul in a life of authenticity. When spiritual practice is unattended, when the call to live a life of integrity is ignored, or when an effort to enter intentionally into union with the divine is deliberately avoided, this is like taking the wide path and is cause for considerable concern.

What about the narrow gate? Like the extremely narrow space of a physical doorsill, the inner threshold has certain imposed limitations. This constricted experience may feel quite confining at first, especially if we are used to traversing thoughtlessly and carelessly through the wide gate. The narrow door enables us to focus on our deepest calling. This focus allows us to collect and weigh what gives our life purpose and direction. As the narrow gate helps us gain clarity, we center more closely on what counts in our life and on what is required from our best self. We learn what is truly essential and worthy of the life to which we are called.

The narrow gate, like a birth canal, has just enough space to squeeze through. This threshold process of birthing includes giving ourselves to what helps us know and live out of our truest, most authentic being. Like a newborn child pushed through the narrow passageway of the mother, or a butterfly formed in the tight space of a chrysalis, or a little chick shaped in the protective, closed-in egg, so the narrow gate brings forth life. Like physical birth, some form of pain often accompanies the advent of spiritual growth.

Jesus warns that few find the narrow door. Again, he uses hyperbole to speak of reality. The road *is* hard that leads to life. It is not easy to be faithful to a life centered on what is required. Christ's teachings on forgiveness, nonjudgment, and compassion rarely lose their challenging nature. The same can be said of fidelity to daily prayer and other spiritual practices.

Healthy spirituality requires balance. Yes, the narrow gate is difficult but that does not mean pain is better than pleasure or that we deliberately seek suffering. Rather, suffering that comes from going through the narrow gate of spiritual transformation is the price to be paid. We accept this reality when we give ourselves to our life's true purpose.

If you look closely, some part of you probably waits on a narrow threshold of unknowing. Some aspect of you rubs its eyes in the fog of elusiveness and presses forward to squeeze through the narrow gate to see beyond where you now are. You may be feeling inner boundaries, the tightness of decision making, the squeezing out of joy through daily difficulties, the pain of not knowing how or when you will step beyond anxiety into peace. You may sense a puzzling lack of clarity about some part of who you are, of how you are to commune with the Holy One, or of how you are to embrace life.

Do not be afraid to go through the narrow gate. New life awaits you.

Reflect on the following:

What part of you needs to refocus and go through the narrow door?

Meditation

Cut a narrow strip of paper. Hold this in your hand as you reread the verse from Matthew 7:13–14. Feel how slim the narrow strip of paper is. Reflect on what is difficult for you in your desire to grow spiritually.

What distracts and diverts you from this desire? (When do you choose the wide door?) Close your eyes and linger with the Holy One. Ask for what you need in order to choose the narrow door. Touch the thin strip of paper again. Renew your intention to stay near the heart of the Holy One. Write one word or phrase on the piece of paper to confirm your desire. Keep this piece of paper near you throughout the day as a reminder of your renewed yearning.

PRAYER

Wise Teacher,
you insist that the narrow gate
will help me regain my focus
on what is worthy and of greatest value.
I am sorry for the times and ways
I have let my wandering heart
carelessly drift away from you.
I open the door of my heart to you.
I open the door.

SCRIPTURE TO CARRY IN YOUR HEART TODAY:

The gate is narrow and the road is hard that leads to life . . . (Mt 7:14).

GUARDIANS OF THE THRESHOLD

Hallow the endless hallway
of doors lined frame by frame;
guardian of the threshold,
cry out my newfound name.

—JAN RICHARDSON

MYTHOLOGIST JOSEPH CAMPBELL researched and wrote about "guardians of the threshold." These fierce-looking, artistic figures are placed at the doors of ancient buildings to signify their protection of the dark inner sanctum of transformation. Campbell explains:

> That is why the approaches and entrances to temples are flanked and defended by colossal gargoyles: dragons, lions, devil-slayers with drawn swords, resentful dwarfs, winged bulls. These are the threshold guardians to ward away all incapable of encountering the higher silences within.... They illustrate the fact that the devotee at the moment of entry into a temple undergoes a metamorphosis.

If we commit ourselves to what transformation requires, there may well be some gargoyles when we enter the "higher silences" within the temple of our deeper self. They will demand our full cooperation in accepting the requirements for spiritual growth. While the specifics of our personal journeys differ, the common factor of transformation is that we can no longer remain just as we are. We are required to change, sometimes radically, when we cross over the threshold. No wonder some get scared by the gargoyles at the entrance and do not accept the call to encounter those aspects of self where we probe the deeper mysteries.

Yes, there are dangers when we stand on the threshold of hazy uncertainty and risk the challenge of uncovering our authenticity. The darkness of depression can lead to thoughts of suicide. Confused haziness leaves one distraught and unable to find energy for daily tasks. Long silences and insecurity can unbalance and deceive with strange delusions.

The good news is that there are also invisible, defending guides to aid us in crossing the threshold. We do not have to make this journey by ourselves. In fact, it may be impossible to do so. When Joseph Campbell warns of the scary gargoyles, he also extends courage to the inner traveler by pointing out legends and myths filled with protective figures like diminutive old women or men who appear at the right time to give counsel, direction, and hope to the threshold journeyer. Among these, Campbell includes the southwestern Navajo Spider Woman, a grandmotherly figure who gives travelers a hoop with feathers to guard themselves, and "the helpful crone and the fairy godmother" of European traditions who provide wisdom and protection.

In my own Roman Catholic tradition, guidance and protection is sought from the Holy Spirit, from Mary the mother of Christ, the saints, (both the canonized and other virtuous ancestors), and in the guardian angels of scriptural tradition. These guardians come in unexpected ways. A woman wrote to tell me of a dream she had during a time when she was struggling to let go of the home of her family roots. In the dream, she is losing significant blood and comes to a house she cannot see clearly (the foggy liminality of the threshold). From behind a closed door her deceased father and mother come to help her. These two guardian figures of the dream offered her encouragement and hope.

The interior journey is nigh impossible to make without gathering strength and inspiration from those who have made the passage before us. Whatever the type of protective figures, we count on them to be with us during our threshold entries into darkness and gestatory waiting. As Methodist minister Jan Richardson so wisely observes, these protective figures cry out our "newfound name," a cry that bespeaks hope, for they believe in the profound change possible for us, if we give ourselves in trust to the process.

Today I invite you to look at your past experience of "encountering the higher silences within" and any trepidation you might have about continuing to enter the deeper recesses of your soul. As you do so, I hope you will recall those who have been guardians of your threshold times and offer them your gratitude.

REFLECT ON THE FOLLOWING:
Who have been some of the invisible, protective guides of your threshold experiences?

MEDITATION
Sit quietly with your attention focused on the in-and-out pattern of your breath. As you breathe in, whisper, "You are with me." As you breathe out, whisper, "I am with you." When you are ready, visualize a sacred dwelling place with dim lighting. See yourself standing before this holy place. On either side of you is a guardian to guide and protect you. Enter the sacred dwelling place and find an enriching sense of peace. Stay there for as long as you wish. When you leave the sacred dwelling place, renew your desire to give your entire self to the Holy One and to the journey of your growth.

PRAYER
Divine Guardian of the Threshold,
your wisdom and guidance
protect and support me in the darkness.
Your love is stronger than my fear.
Your hope is greater than my doubt.
Keep me aware of your presence
as I seek and find my way.
I open the door of my heart to you.
I open the door.

SCRIPTURE TO CARRY IN YOUR HEART TODAY:
I am going to send an angel in front of you, to guard you on the way . . . (Ex 23:20).

WEEK 4, DAY 5

WAITING IN THE DOORWAY

This is not the sudden opening of a door....
—NEIL DOUGLAS-KLOTZ

TIMING IS EVERYTHING. We cannot, and ought not, stay on the threshold forever. On the other hand, we have to be there long enough for our awakening to occur. Waiting in the sphere of uncertainty and confusion challenges even the heartiest of souls. Most often, it is difficult to ascertain just when the appropriate time comes to take that bold step toward departure and move on with our life.

In Week 3, Day 5, we reflected on how some of us try to hurry our gestation. We do not want to wait for the unfolding of our growth. Given our Western culture of "instant everything," waiting is not something most of us accept with ease. We expect what we envision to occur *now*.

Our spiritual eyes adjust gradually to the womb-like darkness of the threshold. Mark Nepo puts it this way in *The Book of Awakening*: "It seems whatever the door, whatever our fear—be it love or truth or even the prospect of death—we all have this choice, again and again: avoiding that part of our house, or opening the door and finding out more about ourselves by waiting until what is dark becomes seeable."

A friend of mine lost his job not long before his young wife died. His search for employment took him through three jobs. His grief over his spouse's death drew him to the dark place of the threshold where he stayed in that lost, frustrating space during the lengthy period he tried to find a job suited to his professional skills. Whenever he bemoaned, "Will I ever get on with my life?" I heard underneath his words, "Will I ever get beyond the threshold?" He desperately wanted an internal place of peace and an external world of success, but it was much too soon for those things. His acute grief and unemployment honed his heart. They humbled him and deepened his compassion for others who stand on similar thresholds.

If we are to grow, we stay in the "holding pattern" of the threshold until we gain its lessons for life and the inner self develops enough stamina to move on. Usually we are unaware of the value of this in-between space until we pass beyond it. A woman who participated in one of my weekend retreats told me she wanted to come to a retreat I gave a year earlier but her schedule did not allow it. She eventually realized that if she had come at that time, she would not have been mentally or emotionally ready. This retreatant did not know it at the time but she had significant psychological work to do regarding an old message of her past. Her growth depended on this gestation. The waiting period prepared her for when her schedule finally opened and she was able to make the retreat. Timing *is* everything.

A pilgrim who walked the long trek of the Camino across northern Spain wrote to tell me about her experience of waiting. She explained that her central reason for making the pilgrimage was to "discover what God wanted" of her. Six months after returning she still did not feel she had received an answer. What she did know is that she had changed somewhat and was continuing to sense expansion of what she had gleaned during those many days of walking. Even though she was not present on the physical path of the pilgrimage any longer, she remained on the threshold of transformation. There was obviously more to learn from the journey begun in Spain. She simply had to wait. The truth was not going to be revealed in her prescribed time.

I've often wondered about certain gospel stories like the Canaanite woman who begs healing for her daughter. Jesus deliberately makes her wait to receive this gift. He also takes his time getting to the gravesite to raise his dear friend Lazarus from the dead. At the wedding feast in Cana, Jesus dilly-dallies around before consenting to his mother's request to change water into wine. Could the symbolism of these biblical stories be to remind us that only when our deeper self is ready will the grace of transformation take place? Do the stories also point to the divine as the vital source of our transformation?

In this regard, James Finley has insightful words for us:

In time the conversion process—in which you learn to identify less and less with your superficial self and more and more with your deep self, one with God—will mature and come to fulfillment. Be patient. Trust that God's generosity is at work, bringing you to a realized oneness with God infinitely beyond anything you might have imagined possible.

This is the ultimate result of opening the door and spending time on the threshold. Immense gifts of growth come to us if we patiently wait for them.

REFLECT ON THE FOLLOWING:

What do you find most difficult about waiting when you are on a threshold?

MEDITATION

Sit in silence. Remember you are not alone. The Holy One is with you. Bring the greatest longings of your heart to this beloved presence. Do nothing after this except wait. Turn your waiting into a hopeful vigil. Let yourself be in this interior posture for at long as you can. When you conclude your meditation, take pen and paper and write: *I wait for....*

PRAYER

Source of Transformation,
you wait with me in the silence.
You are my faith-filled eyes in the dark.
Slow me down when I want to hurry.
Draw me close to you when I try to run.
Teach me how to be patient and wise
when I wait on the threshold of growth.
I open the door of my heart to you.
I open the door.

SCRIPTURE TO CARRY IN YOUR HEART TODAY:

... For you I wait all day long (Ps 25:5).

Week 4, Day 6

Choices to Be Made

Who we become, depends upon the choices we make.
At particular times in our lives, really significant choices
are made that shape our fate.
When we are in a threshold time,
what we decide to do determines what comes next.
—Jean Shinoda Bolen

When we stand on the threshold, eventually this sacred space becomes a time to discern and make decisions about what will most benefit our spiritual growth. As we wait in the liminal space of uncertainty regarding our evolving self and our developing relationship with God, we choose what will bring our best self into further wholeness or we choose what keeps us confined and limited. When we choose only what eases our fear, we lose out. By doing this, we nail our feet to the threshold facing the past. This keeps our inmost self from engaging in the truth that sets us free. With this choice, a part of us gets lost, becomes an orphan of ongoing apprehension hiding us from the home of our authentic self.

One of the tough parts of the threshold comes when we know we must make a choice of how we are going to proceed with our life. So often these choices are made while it is still unclear as to how that choice will grow and set us free. Something in us pulls back from what cannot be proven or assessed as definite. Our heart wants to cling to the known and secure. Will we trust in our true self and our loving Guide? Are we willing to hold our fear gently and step beyond the threshold?

James Finley creates a tender story to illustrate the challenge and pain we go through in making a choice to grow. He asks his readers to imagine a little girl on the day she is to begin kindergarten. She cries because she does not want to leave home. Her wailing and tears tug at her parents' hearts. They would like to give in to her fears and end her crying by telling her she can stay home, but they know this is not in the best interest of their beloved child. The loving parents listen and respond to her concerns. They reassure their child that she will do fine once she discovers the fun she has in new friends and the wonderful things she will learn. Then they take their child to school.

Finley compares this moment to the "little child of our ego self" being sent off to enter another stage of transformation that is essential for spiritual maturity. "This tender point of encounter," Finley writes, "is . . . God in our midst, listening, loving, and helping his children across the threshold into eternal oneness with God."

The choices we are asked to make at the threshold are not so much about what job to take, which home to buy, how much money to save, or when to retire. These are important and can influence spiritual growth, but the selections on the threshold are deeper and more far-reaching. These choices stretch from the soul and into the heart of God. What we decide determines if we will develop innate qualities like compassion, unconditional love, trustworthiness, honesty, other-centeredness, and generosity.

"Whether or not it seems sacred at first," comments Jan Richardson, "a threshold can become a holy place of new beginnings as we tend it, wait within it, and discern the path beyond." Our new beginnings depend on how willing we are to tend the threshold experience and on the choices we eventually make. When we stop fighting the unknown and allow ourselves to linger within it patiently, we will gradually recognize and make decisions that further our transformation.

The central choice at the threshold focuses on these questions: "In deciding what to do with my life, will I choose what activates and refuels my dormant goodness? Will it help me become a loving presence in the world?" If we choose a life in which we use the best of who we are, our choice will ask a lot from us. We will not be able to hide out in self-indulgence or ignore the world's pain. At the same time, this vital choice to live a life reflective of oneness with Eternal Love will result in the heartfelt satisfaction of living the best of our authentic self.

Your finest qualities faithfully wait for you to bring them to life. Welcome them today.

Reflect on the following:

What is the biggest choice you now face? How do you see this choice affecting your authenticity and your relationship with the Holy One?

Meditation

Place your hands over your heart. Remember the indwelling presence of Eternal Love. Bring to mind some aspect of your life in which you are being asked to make a choice to be more than you now are. (More forgiving? Kinder? Accepting? Patient? Truthful? Trusting? Understanding? Caring? Joyful?) Pay attention to your hesitations and fears. Open your mind and heart to the Holy One. Listen for assurance on how to activate more of your hidden goodness. Reflect on how your choice can influence the future. End your meditation by renewing your trust in Holy Wisdom's guidance.

Prayer

Blessed Assurance,
turn me toward your presence
when my concerns try to turn me away.
Move my mind, heart, and will
to make choices that bring forth
the goodness secreted within my self.
Although hesitations push me backward,
with your help I can move forward.
I open the door of my heart to you.
I open the door.

Scripture to carry in your heart today:

Teacher, what good deed must I do to have eternal life? (Mt 19:16).

Week 4, Day 7

Review and Rest

This is your day to gather what has taken place for you during the past week of using this book. It is also meant to be a day of rest for you. Let this reflection and integration time be a gentle pause in your week. (You might choose to read the Introduction to the next week's prayer in the evening of this day or wait and begin fresh the next day, reading it at that time.)

Begin

"A Prayer for Openness" (page 13).

Review

Look back over the week. If you wrote in your journal, review what you've written. If you did not write, sit quietly for a few minutes and let your reflections from this week visit you. Then, respond in writing to the following:

1. The most helpful part of the past week's reflection and prayer was . . .
2. The most challenging part of the past week's reflection and prayer was . . .
3. I want to remember . . .
4. I hope that . . .
5. I wonder . . .

Complete your reflection with a one- or two-line summary of your experience from the week. An alternative to writing might be to summarize the week by drawing, sculpting, creating music, dancing, or using some other form of alternative expression to gather and integrate the week's experience into your present situation.

Another alternative to writing would be to summarize each week by drawing a door. Place words, phrases, drawings, or other symbols on the door to depict what happened within the week to draw you into further growth. (Instead of drawing a door, you could post these words, etc., on a real door in your home.)

CONCLUDE

Close with one of the prayers from the week and/or by sitting quietly for a few minutes of gratitude.

Week 5

Closing the Door

INTRODUCTION

A wise counselor once said to me
that the ability to close some doors,
never to open them again,
is one of the principal signs of maturity.
—ROBERT P. MALONEY

YOU MIGHT BE inclined to wonder why this week centers on closing doors when I have been encouraging you to open them. Here is the reason: we cannot move forward unless we are willing to leave something behind. The wise poet, Jalaluddin Rumi, understood the necessity of this movement. In one of his poems, Rumi notes how a closed fist precedes the opening of a hand. If the hand is always open or closed, the hand is crippled. Rumi then draws a parallel to spiritual movement:

> So your heart contracts and expands,
> just like a bird needs to close and open
> its wings and fly.

There is a time to open and a time to close the door. If we are going to fly freely and step deeply into our soul in order to live with greater consciousness, certain doors have to be closed. When we stand on the threshold, we will be there forever until we make a decision to either go forward or turn around and go back. With either decision, we leave something behind. Sometimes closing a door is exactly the choice to make because it frees us to enter a fresh dimension of growth. At other times, closing the door is the worst choice because the closure blocks our growth and keeps us trapped.

Some closed doors paralyze our ability to mature. They prevent us from moving toward further exploration and activation of our authentic self. Unresolved anger results in blocking our peace. Likewise, when we harbor old hurts we slam the door shut instead of searching for the doorknob to find a way out of our pain. Refusing to pardon ourselves for our failures is another obstruction to growth. Country-western singer Johnny

Cash once said this about his own mishaps: "Close the door on the past. You don't try to forget the mistakes, but you don't dwell on it. You don't let it have any of your energy, or any of your time, or any of your space."

When I spoke about closing doors with a friend who is a recovering alcoholic, he led me to the "Big Book," *Alcoholics Anonymous*. He pointed out a section advising those in recovery "to know a new freedom and a new happiness . . . to not regret the past nor wish to shut the door on it." My friend told me he was puzzled by this message. As I reflected on the section, it seemed that my friend was being encouraged to close the door to drinking, but not shut out what his disease had taught him. If he forgot his past behavior or his old way of thinking, he might slip into drinking again. When we close a door to our past, it does not mean that the memories or "lessons" are forsaken. Rather, we take with us what is beneficial for our growth.

The central theme of this week focuses on closing doors in order to help, not hinder, our transformational process. What do we step away from in order to be more fully our true self? What is it we are to leave behind so our communion with the Holy One grows in constancy and trustworthiness? When is it time to cross the threshold, close the door behind us, and move on to mine the treasures we have yet to claim?

When it comes to closing the door, some people hurry too fast. Some dawdle way too long. Others muster up courage and manage to bring the necessary closure in an adequate amount of time. Whatever our tendency, we usually sense a readiness within us to move away from the past and enter a new phase of growth. We notice how a situation, or a way of being that was helpful to us, gradually confines our personal development. Even though some part of us tugs at staying put, deep down we realize the time is ripe to shut the door and go forward. When a hurt has been healed, a difficulty resolved, a love restored or ended, a sense of self-worth renewed, a grief subsided, a constricted spirit relaxed, we close the door and move on.

In reviewing the central stories in both the Jewish and Christian scriptures, I see this closure occurring repeatedly. Abraham and Sarah heed God's call to gather up their belongings, close the door to what they have known, and advance into nomadic territory. None of the healing and teachings of Jesus would have blessed others had he been unwilling to depart from the security of Nazareth and set out for the risky territory of his public ministry. Little development of the early church would have taken place if the Spirit had not encouraged the disciples to move beyond their fears and distress after the death of Jesus.

Some basic requirements are necessary for closing doors. These essentials enable us to let go and travel toward the prospect of what is yet to be revealed. Take a look at the following. You may think of other prerequisites to add to the list.

Intention:
Deliberately decide to close the door. Renew this intention daily.

Resolution:
Be determined that, with God's help and guidance, the door *can* be closed.

Clearing:
Ensure that nothing blocks the door's ability to be shut. Remove what keeps the opening obstructed.

Strength:
Count on inner resiliency and courage to get the door closed.

Hope:
Believe with all your heart that it is possible to move forward. Have a steadfast aspiration of being able to travel beyond what is known.

Gratitude:
Remember that knowledge and valued experience come from what you leave behind. This wisdom gives impetus toward the next stage of growth.

This week I invite you to ponder the entryway to life, knowing that this doorway requires some dying or relinquishment in order to yield its fruitfulness. Be aware of the physical doors you close each day. Notice how shutting a door gives you entrance into another space while it also closes you out from the area you leave behind. Go through the coming days with your hand in the hand of the Holy One, knowing you have this marvelous assistance to help you push some doors shut before you open others.

WEEK 5, DAY 1

STEPPING INSIDE

As often happens on the spiritual journey,
we have arrived at the heart of a paradox:
each time a door closes,
the rest of the world opens up.
—PARKER PALMER

WHEN WE CROSS the inner threshold and close the door behind us, we enter the deeper terrain of our being. We "step inside" our heart. Once we do this, writes Parker Palmer, we are able to explore "the largeness of life that now lies open to our souls." With this crossing, he notes, "what now lies before us is the rest of reality."

A good portion of this reality resides in the beauty and bounty of our essence. Saint Teresa of Avila describes our inner being as one containing the "good qualities" of our souls and (God) who dwells within them. Here lies the real shape and character of our genuine self and the One who gifts us with this identity. Each closing of one door and opening of another invites us to receive greater awareness.

A pastoral associate in a large parish was forced to close the door to her cherished ministry after Multiple Sclerosis impeded her mobility. She related how this closure was leading the way inward: "In the quietness of

WEEK FIVE: Closing the Door   121

my home, I can learn interior silence and cultivate a contemplative spirit. I have time to read and reflect. I have left active ministry, but I can continue to serve by praying for the people and ministries that I loved."

Joan Chittister hails the value of moving on in *The Story of Ruth:*

> Change points are those moments in life in which we get inside ourselves to find out that we are not, at the end, really one person at all. We are many—each of them lying in wait to come to life. We are each a composite of experiences and abilities, of possibilities and hopes, of memories and wonder, of gifts and wishes. Every stage of life calls on a different dimension of the self. Every stage of life is another grace of being that teaches us something new about ourselves, that demands something sterner of ourselves, that enables us to learn something deeper about our God.

A colleague in the midst of a significant spiritual transition commented to me one day, "The first step of closing the door is the hardest." He then spoke about his fear of accepting the possible change that entering into deeper union with God might ask of him. "Changing," he groaned, "is great to talk about but tough to do."

In his memoir *Local Wonders,* Ted Kooser comments on this struggle to welcome change's unknown factors: "We are always trying to find footing on the damp edge of the future, but to most of us, the dry sand of the past feels firmer under our sneakers." This is so true. Yet, if we are to grow, we eventually leave "the dry sand of the past" behind us.

Part of the challenge in the spiritual life is that there is never just one door to close. We open and shut many of them throughout life. The pattern repeats itself over and over: Open the door, close the door, open the door, close the door. . . . This rhythm is reflected in a poem by Gunilla Norris. She addresses the Holy One as she reflects on how she locks the door of her home at night and unlocks it every morning. Each of her days contains this rhythm of locking and unlocking, which Norris calls "a pulse." She concludes her reflection with these lines:

> I can dwell in this home
> as if it were a heart. When I feel that pulse
> I know that all that comes to me will also go.
> Living in this stream I understand

You are my life blood. Let me feel
You course through me, through this door,
throughout my life.

Today, get in touch with the inner rhythm of your life, the opening and closing of doors that allow you to know yourself better and to strengthen your union with the Holy One.

Reflect on the following:

How do you experience the spiritual rhythm of opening and closing doors?

Meditation

Let yourself relax in the assurance of God's presence. Step inside your heart by being as quiet as possible. Count down from ten to one as you take steps down into your secret self. When you get to one, look at your inner world as if you are looking into a vast treasure box filled with jewels of many shapes and colors. These beautiful jewels symbolize your essence. Rejoice at what you see. Then join your heart to the Holy One and spend some time in trusting, grateful communion.

Prayer

Treasure of My Heart,
you have placed within me
what I need to be a person of great love.
I have the ability to close any doors
that keep me from finding this inner treasure.
Help me step inside my heart each day
and to let go of what keeps me from you.
I open the door of my heart to you.
I open the door.

I will give you the treasures of darkness and riches hidden in secret places ... (Is 45:3).

Week 5, Day 2

Leaving Behind

As one door is closed in your life
a new one opens before you.
Pause briefly at this threshold
and know that what you are leaving behind
is for the best....
—M.E. Miro

NOT LONG AGO, I came across some musty journal notes I wrote fourteen years ago. I penned them during a significant period of closing and opening doors when I met with a Jungian therapist for two years. This included vital decision making about my way of life and how I view myself. During those years, I left behind a part of my past and embraced the person I hoped to become. The notes I found were a response to some questions that Maria Harris asks in *Jubilee Time*. She queries: "What do you wish to tear up ... to give away ... to burn ... to remove ... to plant ... to sing ... to create ... to wear?" Here is how I responded to those questions:

> I am tearing up old behavioral patterns of judging others, being too busy and anxious, of not having enough solitude and communion with the earth. I want to give away whatever keeps me from being my true self, from living freely and simply, from being rooted in God. I wish to burn old memories and experiences that wound myself and

others. I want to remove any obstacle that keeps me from being a loving woman. I long to plant seeds of kindness, a deep reverence for our planet, a healthy spirituality, to plant these seeds in myself and in all I meet. I want to sing the song of my soul, to create the books waiting in my heart, to wear freedom and love.

As I reviewed those old responses, I thought about who I am now. The changes I hoped for are gradually happening, but only because I left some things behind. During that time of decision making, I deliberately chose to not carry old wounds and unloving patterns across the threshold into the future. Because of this, I *am* different than I was back then. The song of my soul *does* resonate more easily. Peace *has* become a regular resident within my life.

My growth did not stop with that experience of leaving behind. Since writing those notes, I've had other closures to encourage my growing. I have little doubt that this process will continue as I age, as I open the door to other challenging life encounters. There will never be an end to closing doors and leaving some things behind, just as there will never be an end to moving through the open doorway to greater freedom.

Robert Wicks acknowledges the value of closing the door and saying farewell to certain parts of our past in his book *Crossing the Desert:* "We must be willing to constantly sit on the edge of mystery and *un*learn what has helped guide us in the past but is no longer as useful now. To do this we must be willing to ask the questions that will open us up to hear the quiet, powerful voice of freedom."

A part of us wants to grow and a part of us resists. The thought of freedom is attractive, but *unlearning* rattles the chains of our captured past. Yet, we cannot move on without being willing to yield and let go. We simply must slip out of our tenacious grasp on what prevents our growth.

This unlearning includes leaving behind regrets and self-blame over what we did or did not do, learned patterns of response when we are hurt or betrayed, old messages that taunt our self-worth, ego tricks that urge us to feel superior and overly important, false expectations of self or others, beliefs and theories we guarded carefully but now prove to be limp and useless. These and anything else that keeps us from discovering and sharing the treasure of our inner goodness must be left behind.

I invite you to take the growth-filled questions Maria Harris asks and respond to them. Browse through your learned attitudes and behaviors. Look at who you are and how you "do" life in the light of doors that may need closing.

REFLECT ON THE FOLLOWING:

"What do you wish to tear up . . . to give away . . . to burn . . . to remove . . . to plant . . . to sing . . . to create . . . to wear?"

MEDITATION

Deliberately close a door in your room or home before this meditation as a sign of your willingness to leave behind what keeps you from activating more of who you are. Then sit down and become aware of the Holy One's presence. Ask God to help you in your yielding process. Mentally place whatever you need to leave behind in your open hands. Hold it quietly with the deliberate desire of releasing it. Make an intention to send it on its way. Close your meditation by gently receiving the Holy One's blessing. After this, go and open a door and stand in its spaciousness with a hopeful heart.

PRAYER

Beloved of My Soul,
at every door I open and close
you accompany me with your love.
Your voice of freedom urges me onward.
Teach me what I need to unlearn
and what I must leave behind.
With your help, I take courageous steps forward.
I open the door of my heart to you.
I open the door.

Everything old has passed away; see, everything has become new (2 Cor 5:17).

WEEK 5, DAY 3

EXPERIENCING LOSS

When suffering knocks at your door
and you say there is no seat for him,
he tells you not to worry
because he has brought his own stool.

—CHINUA ACHEBE

WHEN WE CLOSE the door to what was once a learned part of our self, discomfort, uneasiness, and a sense of loss may afflict us. The decisions we make can disappoint others and even bring about their ridicule or rejection. We may find ourselves having to guard our solitude, risk the possible loss of a job, or struggle with a valued relationship. Self-doubt, guilt about moving on, questions about the timing, and fear of an inability to close the door often arise.

When we let go, we put something to rest. We choose to no longer have it be readily available to us. Jesus spoke about this graced action to his disciples. In John's gospel, he tells them that a grain of wheat has to "fall to the ground and die" if it is going to produce "much fruit." If the wheat seed does not die, it will never bring about new life (Jn 12:24–26). The wheat falling into the ground and dying is another way of saying "this door has to be closed before another one opens."

The story Jesus used with his disciples comprises the nucleus of spiritual transformation. If we want spiritual growth, dyings or endings go along with it. A seed stays a seed unless its form and state of being change. Like the wheat seed, we give ourselves to the process. Another way Jesus might have told his parable would be: "Amen, Amen, I say to you, unless you close the door to what keeps you from enlarging your capacity to grow, unless you let go of what keeps your view of self too small, you will hold yourself back from becoming who you truly are."

As the grain of wheat falls to the ground, it lets go of what it is for what it can become. When we close the door to a part of who we believed we were, or to a part of what our life is like, we open the way for another aspect of self to emerge. When we take the step to move on, it becomes possible to generate "fruit" that would not have been produced had we stayed within the confinement and refuge of who we thought we were.

Closing a door, leaving behind, letting go, surrendering—these spiritual movements include suffering of some type. Even if it is something we have long wanted to let go of, like a strong memory of a wounded experience, the painful memory of that wound will resurface as we go through the process of closing the door. Likewise, when we first attempt to resuscitate a part of our inner goodness, such as our ability to be generous, the pain of recognizing how ungenerously we have lived humbles us until this quality becomes an integrated part of our daily expression.

Inayat Khan, the beloved Sufi master who originated the *Dances of Universal Peace,* remarked that "the heart sleeps until it is awakened to life by a blow." One impact that rouses our heart occurs when we do not have a choice about closure. The door slams shut and, try as we will, we cannot force it open again. This harsh closure happens with a misfortune such as an unexpected announcement of divorce, a job loss, a diagnosis of severe illness, or the sudden death of a loved one. The life event forces us to let go of what we thought we had. Unwanted endings also take place when a statement or experience rips apart the bias and underpinnings that once gave credence to an accepted belief. These closures painfully expose the false foundation of our supposed certainty.

Like the grain of wheat in the ground, we may not see how we are growing and changing until long after a great force has swept away what provided sanctuary for us. We will walk with the emptiness of leaving behind, taste the soreness of lonely resistance, and wait in the hollows of our inner poverty until deeper meaning surfaces.

During this soreness of spirit, our sense of the divine often alters and surprises us with a depth we did not know before. We close the door, breathe in a gust of grace, and realize that, oh yes, this divine life in us is more than we once thought or imagined it could be.

REFLECT ON THE FOLLOWING:

What suffering do I most fear when the door closes?

MEDITATION

If you have a living plant in your home, hold this plant or sit beside it. Reflect on the loss the plant went through in order to be what it is today (the seed in darkness, waiting for growth, dependence on another to care for it . . .). If you do not have a plant, read John 12:23–25. Reflect on the wheat seed's journey from death to life. Ask the Holy One to teach you about a loss you have experienced, to see how it led to growth. At the conclusion of the meditation, renew your commitment to respond positively to door-closings that enrich your growth and strengthen your relationship with God.

PRAYER

Source of Transformation,
there are seeds of new life
hidden in my deepest self.
Let me not run from the loss
that enables these seeds to grow.
Help me access my resilience and courage
so I enter into the dyings that bring life.
I open the door of my heart to you.
I open the door.

The sufferings of this present time are not worth comparing with the glory about to be revealed in us (Rom 8:18).

WEEK 5, DAY 4

SHUTTING THE DOOR

But whenever you pray,
go into your room
and shut the door and pray
to your Father who is in secret.
—MATTHEW 6:6

SHUTTING THE DOOR to the outside world in order to spend time alone with the Holy One is another indispensable aspect of door-closing. When we close the door to external activity, we pause to be in solidarity with the One who enriches and restores our inner balance. We give ourselves to silent communion with our divine guide who leads us to the richness of our authentic self and encourages us to share this goodness with others. Jesus wisely left behind the pressing crowds to find solitude for prayer and encouraged others to do the same. Deliberately separating from the world's hurried pace nourishes our soul and keeps us spiritually alert. We gain perspective on our concerns, develop awareness of how we allow thoughts and feelings to take over, and restore our ability to not give in to unhealthy cravings.

Thomas Merton longed for this prayerful solitude. Even though he was a Trappist monk, he had to make a concerted effort to find an undisturbed place for himself. Merton firmly believed in the value of shutting the door:

There should be at least a room, or some corner where
will find you and disturb you or notice you. You should be
untether yourself from the world and set yourself free, loo
the fine strings and strands of tension that bind you, by si
sound, by thought, to the presence of other [people]. ... Once you
have found such a place, be content with it, and do not be disturbed
if a good reason takes you out of it. Love it, and return to it as soon
as you can, and do not be quick to change it for another.

Saint Teresa of Avila insisted on the necessity of closing the door to
the outside world for a while in order to enter our interior life: ". . . the
door of entry into this castle is prayer and meditation." Beatrice Bruteau,
founder of Schola Contemplationis, concludes similarly when she supports
the value of solitude:

Shutting the door again means refusing distractions or finite
identifications, silencing the mind. . . . You need to go deeply and
secretly into your inner chamber and seek your Source . . . Let
us learn also to turn the mind inward, to enter into our "inner
chamber and shut the door" so as to seek the root of our being in
secret. When the secret root has been found, it will show, for our
life will be transformed.

All this sounds extremely valuable and, yet, when it comes to putting
theory into practice, how difficult to shut the door and seek our Source of
Love. A friend of mine, a highly successful businessman in great demand
for his skilled services, kept sensing a pull inward toward stillness. A part
of him longed to close the door on his thriving and highly productive life,
to become less active and more reflective. After several frustrating years of
struggling with this yearning and of trying to explain his choices to col-
leagues, he finally found the courage to retire early, close the door to what
had given external worth to his life, and open the door to a more contemplative mode of being. Out of his struggle "to close the door and pray in
secret" came not only a deeper life with God, but a surprisingly fertile creativity. Today my friend's amazing art and evocative poetry bound forth
from his satisfied contemplative soul.

Sufi teacher Neil Douglas-Klotz suggests a lovely way to approach
closing the door to the outside world to ensure time for inner communion.

He refers to prayer as "the enclosure of the divine creativity." Douglas-Klotz remarks that this closure is "not like shutting a door" so much as it is "like gradually folding the wings of love around us." What a tender way to describe going apart to pray!

I leave you today with this question of Wayne Muller's: "What if the answers to our questions about life and path and practice are already speaking to us, and in our rush to find them elsewhere we miss the easy, gentle wisdom that would teach us all we need to know if we simply center ourselves and be still for just a moment?"

REFLECT ON THE FOLLOWING:

What doors require closing in order for you to have adequate time to pray in solitude?

MEDITATION

Once again, close a physical door before you begin your meditation. Do so with deliberate intention as you prepare to enter the secret room of your heart and be alone with the Source of Love. As you sit, be attentive to the rhythm of your breath, going in and out. Then focus on the Holy One who is the Opener and the Closer. Give your heart to this beloved presence. Imagine the Holy One enfolding you with wings of love. Stay in this awareness for as long as you can and when you are ready to conclude your meditation, offer your prayers of love, hope, and gratitude.

PRAYER

Beloved Companion,
you enfold me in your wings of love.
Fill my heart with devotion for you.
Stir up renewed commitment to go apart
and rest my soul in your welcoming presence.
Restore any lost desire for union with you.
Continue to draw me into your embrace.
I open the door of my heart to you.
I open the door.

WEEK 5, DAY 5

THE EXIT DOOR

Death, your servant, is at my door. . . .
It is your messenger who stands at my door.
—RABINDRANATH TAGORE

ONCE WE PASS through certain doors, such as theater exits, we cannot use that door to get back inside again. Physical death is similar to those exits. In due course, the door of death brings finality and completion to bodily existence. Not many people are completely comfortable and accepting of their own demise. In his book on aging, changing, and dying, Ram Dass comments: "We remain a society in which death is viewed as the enemy, an onerous 'thing' to be hidden or shunned, and separated, physically and philosophically, as much as possible from living."

Being a volunteer for Hospice has helped raise my awareness and openness toward my own death. Yet, it is one thing to think about death when it is not immanent and quite another when the diagnosis of a terminal illness, a debilitating depression, or the death of a beloved family member brings death close. Andrew Harvey draws this reality sharply into focus:

> There is a moment when you realize that you are going to have to die in reality, not just pretend to die, not just read about dying, not just recite Rumi late at night, but really, day by day, hour by hour, moment by moment, go into the darkness of the Love of God and really surrender, a moment when you realize that to do that, you will need Divine courage.

No matter how much death might be feared or avoided, eventually we will exit the physical dimension of life. What we do with the impermanent life we now have determines our attitude and approach when we go through the exit door into the mysterious world beyond. "The trust, confidence, and courage that enables us to go through the *little doors* and experience the *little deaths* of daily living somehow rehearse us for the opening of that final door," observed Sister of Loretto Mary Luke Tobin. The sufferings of our daily dyings train and strengthen us for the final moment here on earth. As Tobin indicates, life constantly offers us the opportunity to rehearse going through death's door. Dawna Markova reflects on "practicing for death" in this way:

> When I die, I want to remember the pulse of life. . . . I want to be well practiced in letting go over the edge of the known, holding onto that golden Wonder Woman rope woven of threads of love and feel it untwining into a thousand directions. . . . It's not so much about being prepared for death as it is about being full of life. I want to be so well practiced in crossing thresholds that dying is merely another step in the dance.

Preparing for the exit door of death involves not only learning and growing from our daily dying, but also allowing these times of letting go and surrender to bring us into fuller appreciation of what truly counts in life. The gusto and spirited passion that Markova suggests can be ours as we continue to pass through life's transforming stages.

Lessons of creation and teachings from scripture assure us that life follows death, whether this transformation exists within a seed, a sunset, or a human soul. When this truth of transformation roots itself strongly enough in us, we approach both the daily dyings and the exit door of death with Rabindranath Tagore's hope-filled stance. The poet asks what treasures we will turn over when death comes to the door. He then answers the question:

> I'll bring
> my full soul before him.

A "full soul" implies having relished and celebrated the bounty of one's existence. Today's theme need not dampen joy. Quite the opposite.

Reflecting on the exit door to death puts things in perspective and increases gratitude for the life one has. Notice today what you pay too much attention to and what deserves your appreciation and dedication.

REFLECT ON THE FOLLOWING:

What thoughts and feelings stir as you think about your own "exit door"?

MEDITATION

Remember the nearness of divine presence. Turn your entire being toward this presence, with fullest confidence that you are cared for by an ancient and unending love. Imagine that you have just one year to live. Picture what you would do with that one year; what would you change . . . embrace . . . resolve . . . restore? How would your one year left to live affect your relationship with God? As you conclude your meditation, return again to the Ancient Love dwelling with you. Rest there in peace as you prepare to walk into the day with a renewed awareness of what you most value.

PRAYER

Keeper of My Soul,
your love is stronger than death.
Your assurance is greater than my doubt.
Your grace is richer than my poverty.
Your courage is bolder than my fear.
Your vigilance is longer than my life.
In living and in dying, I entrust myself to you.
I open the door of my heart to you.
I open the door.

SCRIPTURE TO CARRY IN YOUR HEART TODAY:

If the earthly tent we live in is destroyed, we have a building from God, a house not made with hands, eternal in the heavens (2 Cor 5:1).

A SWINGING DOOR

When we become truly ourselves,
we just become a swinging door.
We are purely independent of,
and at the same time, dependent upon everything.
—SHUNRYU SUZUKI

OH, TO BECOME the kind of door that swings with ease between the inner and outer world, to dwell in authenticity so completely that oneness with God and life moves along fluently. For the past five weeks, we focused on the door swinging inward to our heart. This movement offered the possibility of learning more about both the known and the unknown parts of our self. Going within also established increased awareness of the Indwelling One.

When we close the door and enter our gestating heart-space, we choose a temporary invisible boundary to allow independence of what normally claims our time and attention. This liberating process helps uncover our latent goodness and prepares us to integrate and share these worthy traits with others. What we discover and accept in the stillness of our solitude is meant to be brought forth. Once this in-and-out movement becomes well established, our union with the Holy One readily blends into both inner and outer spheres. It is time now for the door of the heart to swing outward where our relationship with the divine also touches every dimension of life.

This external aspect is reflected in a question asked by Hafiz: "Where is the door to God?" In other poems, this Sufi poet writes about finding the divine within our deepest self. Here Hafiz responds to the question by suggesting this door is found everywhere:

In the sound of a barking dog,
In the ring of a hammer,
In a drop of rain,
In the face of
Everyone
I see.

Because our self includes layers of truth and because life continually evolves in an unexpected manner, about the time we are developing an almost effortless rhythm with the swinging door, something comes along to disrupt the flow. This is to be expected. Any minor or major occurrence can influence the rhythm. Events, circumstances, thoughts, feelings, memories can interrupt the movement. Consolation entices us to stay inside too long. Desolation tempts us to move outside too soon. With life's continual gain and loss, welcomes and farewells, the ache of loss seems particularly to pull us away from the external world. As William Stafford notes, grief is never quite done with us:

> Among shirts in their closets with their empty
> sleeves—among coats that embrace only air—
> my old grief hides. Doors close, lights click;
> footsteps count off into silence; and there
> my old grief bows in its corner again.
> It lives on in its quiet, at home in the dark,
> tugging a sleeve sometimes for a word,
> for a gesture, for a warm coat.

In a similar vein, the opposite movement happens. Our culture of extreme extroversion and work-orientation causes us to swing the door outward and lures our focus toward the outside world much longer than is good for our spiritual well-being. No matter whether the inner or outer world tugs on the sleeve of our attention, we ought not lose our balance for too long. We are meant to return, time and again, to the flow of the swinging door so we do not let life's interruptions cause us to falter in our commitment to give and receive love.

Today we swing the door toward the zone of inwardness where we gather the gifts of the heart. Then, we go forth to bring the best of who we are through the heart's swinging door into the marketplace. For there, too, the Beloved One awaits us.

Reflect on the following:

In which direction does the swinging door of your heart tend to get caught? What causes it to stay there?

Meditation

As you pause to be with the Beloved, place your hands over your heart. Allow your focus to be as inward as possible. Let this Love be firmly grounded in you. Dwell with the presence of the Holy One for as long as you can. Then, move your hands from your heart outward in a wide open arc toward the outer world. Again, unite with the Beloved and send the enriching love within you outward to the wider realms of life. After you have reached outward with your love, receive the love coming toward you from the external world. Close your meditation by folding your hands on your lap. Enter into peace.

Prayer

All-Embracing Love,
you are the equilibrium of my life.
When I lean too strongly toward the outer world
draw me back to silence and solitude.
When I cling too firmly to my inner world,
urge me forth to share what you have given.
Move me always in the direction of growth.
I open the door of my heart to you.
I open the door.

Scripture to carry in your heart today:

If we live by the Spirit, let us also be guided by the Spirit (Gal 5:25).

Week 5, Day 7

Review and Rest

This is your day to gather what has taken place for you during the past week of using this book. It is also meant to be a day of rest for you. Let this reflection and integration time be a gentle pause in your week. (You might choose to read the Introduction to the next week's prayer in the evening of this day or wait and begin fresh the next day, reading it at that time.)

Begin
"A Prayer for Openness" (page 13).

Review
Look back over the week. If you wrote in your journal, review what you've written. If you did not write, sit quietly for a few minutes and let your reflections from this week visit you. Then, respond in writing to the following:

1. The most helpful part of the past week's reflection and prayer was . . .
2. The most challenging part of the past week's reflection and prayer was . . .
3. I want to remember . . .
4. I hope that . . .
5. I wonder . . .

Complete your reflection with a one- or two-line summary of your experience from the week. An alternative to writing might be to summarize the week by drawing, sculpting, creating music, dancing, or using some other form of alternative expression to gather and integrate the week's experience into your present situation.

Another alternative to writing would be to summarize each week by drawing a door. Place words, phrases, drawings, or other symbols on the door to depict what happened within the week to draw you into further growth. (Instead of drawing a door, you could post these words, etc., on a real door in your home.)

CONCLUDE

Close with one of the prayers from the week and/or by sitting quietly for a few minutes of gratitude.

Week 6

Beyond the Door

INTRODUCTION

We and the world interpenetrate.
We are in the world like salt in the ocean.
I myself am my own unique door to the world
and in a sense the world is the door to myself.
—JAMES FINLEY

AT ONE OF my favorite retreat centers, a special gesture moves my heart at the close of the eucharistic liturgy. The director goes to the front of the chapel which contains a tall, glass wall looking out onto the forest. She slides open the transparent door in the center of the wall and stands in the doorway facing out. We all join her in extending our outstretched arms to the world beyond the trees. As we do so, the director voices the sending forth of peace to nearby neighbors, to loved ones, to those who call us enemy, to those whom we call enemy, to the suffering, the poor, and to all those yearning for peace. The eucharistic gift we received stirs and expands in our hearts as our outstretched arms present this love to the extended creation. Tears often fill my eyes because this reaching-out gesture and its accompanying prayer so visibly displays how the inner and outer worlds are truly interlocked and bound together.

Whether we open the door of our heart to the larger world at the close of a worship service, the end of personal meditation, the conclusion of faith-sharing, or after an experience of inner awakening, the heart's door is meant to be opened outward. We lean into the breeze of the external realm, extend the peace and divine communion given us when we opened the door inward, and offer these gifts to the larger dimension of life.

In one of Ranier Maria Rilke's many beautiful poems, he speaks to God with these words:

> I don't want to think of a place for you.
> Speak to me from everywhere....
> When I go toward you
> it is with my whole life.

When we leave the inner chamber of our deeper self, we continue to go toward the Holy One with our whole life. Barbara Brown Taylor, an Episcopal priest, affirms this when she writes:

> Church is not a stopping place but a starting place for discerning God's presence in this world.... When [people] leave church, they no more leave God than God leaves them. They simply carry what they have learned into the wide, wide world where there is a crying need for people who will recognize the holiness in things and hold them up to God.

A while back, I read with satisfaction a letter to the editor in a future-oriented magazine that focuses on scientific theories related to the mind and consciousness. More recently, the magazine diverted from this inner-oriented approach and published an issue centered on social action and world peace. The letter I read was a response to the outcries of readers who felt the editor forfeited the true nature of the magazine by calling attention to issues of justice. Here is what Gail Jolley wrote:

> Focusing exclusively on one's own self-development leads to selfishness. What is the purpose of it? Is it only so that we can feel good about ourselves? That is a fine first step, but eventually it must go further if it is to do us any good. It must lead to love and acceptance of others, to the recognition that our well-being is connected to the well-being of others, to the desire to help others find the well-being that we have found. It must lead to serving humanity via some constructive effort that we are uniquely qualified to do.

When I read that letter, I wanted to give Jolley a standing ovation. She sums up succinctly where our spiritual practice takes us. If prayer, meditation, and other reflective activities only circle around inside us without the benefit of sharing the gifts we receive, we spiritually suffocate. Not only that, we miss the growth-filled opportunities the outer world promises ourselves and others when we engage with it.

"The world is the door to myself," writes James Finley. When we go through the door into the external dimension of life, this sphere influences our spiritual growth. For here, as with our inner being, the Spirit of love and guidance weaves through all we encounter. Imagine how stunted and undeveloped our inner life would be without the teachings and helpful insights we receive from opening the door to the outer world.

I think of who I would fail to be and the life I would miss were it not for opening the door outward. For here I find kindhearted people whose trust enables me to share my inner goodness. Here is a magnificent universe replete with a vast space of stars, diverse lands and seas filled with mystery, an amazing array of beauty kindling my joy and awe. Here I journey with those who draw me out of my ego-orientation and ignite my dormant other-centeredness by allowing me to be with them in their happiness and sorrow. Here are difficult situations that challenge my peace and force me to see elements of my personality and my shadow that I prefer to avoid. Here the witness and daily steadfastness of caring human beings inspires and encourages me. Here the wisdom and insight of wise mentors and creative visionaries instills hope. Here the world's heartache and misery calls forth my compassionate action. Yes, the world provides a door for my authentic self to engage with the Holy One's transforming presence.

As you move through this last week of opening the door, may the outer realms you enter be affected positively by your being there. Whenever and wherever you go in this external territory, may your passion for life and union with the Holy One encourage greater unity and transformation. Go forth each day from your private sphere of prayer and reflection into this wider world, the one awaiting the blessing of your attention and loving presence. For this place, too, has the potential of drawing you and your relationships ever closer to the divine.

WEEK 6, DAY 1

BRINGING SERVICE

The message was driven home:
when you walk through those doors,
you bring only yourself.
—PAULA D'ARCY

IN *SACRED THRESHOLDS*, Paula D'Arcy tells a story about providing an evening program for women inmates at a nearby prison. Before she left home, Paula received specific instructions about what to do before going through the prison's security system. Consequently, when she arrived at the prison's parking lot, she complied with the instructions in this way:

> I popped the trunk of my car and removed every piece of jewelry, including my watch. I threw in my pocketbook. I removed my car key from a key ring bursting with keys, each one representing entry into the busyness of my life. From my wallet I retrieved my license. It was a strange exercise with a great deal of power. . . . Your education and degrees no longer serve you. No one cares. Your level of income is irrelevant. Your pretenses are dangerous. Nothing will get through the metal detectors but who you really are.

Who we really are. No matter what form of paid or volunteer work, whether actively engaged outside the home or in it, the most valuable gift we bring to this labor is our self. The more we open the door to our depths and learn from what we find there, the greater spiritual richness we are able to bring to others. We go forth humbly, no longer hiding behind the careful defense of our persona. We enter our work knowing there is much to receive from others, as well as give to them. We set out with the power of the Holy One alive and resilient in us, a union that strengthens our sense of self and our ability to bring our inner goodness into our occupation.

When John O'Donohue reflects on the value of work, he, too, acknowledges that it is our deeper self we bring.

> The invisible within us finds a form, and comes to expression. Therefore, our work should be the place where the soul can enjoy becoming visible and present. The rich unknown, reserved and precious within us, can emerge into visible form.

Work changes into service when we view it as more than something that has to be done, when it becomes a way for our authentic self to transmit integrity, kindness, and justice to our world. Gregory Pierce defines the spirituality of work as "a disciplined attempt to align ourselves and our environment with God and to incarnate God's spirit in the world through the efforts (paid and unpaid) we exert to make the world a better place, a little closer to the way God would have things."

When we bring *who we really are* to our work, we may sometimes feel inadequate or unworthy. Carol Orsborn takes this sense of inadequacy into account when she reflects on what she has to offer to the world. She does not let it get in the way of her desire and decision to serve.

> I fall short of my own ideals over and over. Yet, despite the certainty of my unworthiness, I feel spirit urging me to venture forth again.
>
> So, God, I ask you to use me, anyway.
> Take my fears and use me, anyway.
> Take my failures and use me, anyway.
> Take my arrogance and use me, anyway.
> Take my greed and use me, anyway.
> Take my guilt and use me, anyway.
> Take my confusion and use me, anyway.
> Take my regret and use me, anyway.
> I offer all of myself to you.
> Use me to serve many or few.
> In pain or in joy.
> Use me as you will.

Jesus did not call perfect people to join him in his ministry. None of us is faultless. A huge amount of work in our world begs to be done with an attitude of care. Let us go to be of service to others with our strengths *and* our limitations, trusting that God will take the best of who we are and bless others with it.

REFLECT ON THE FOLLOWING:

How much of what you do each day is service and what part is just plain work?

MEDITATION

Stand in an open doorway. Take a deep breath and deliberately unite with the Holy One's presence. Call to mind the inner qualities you bring with you into your labors. Extend your arms outward beyond the door. As you do so, send forth your earnest love toward those who are a part of your life today. Imagine this love blessing them. Continue standing in the doorway. Now extend your love to the larger world. Face the East. Send your love to this part of the world. Do the same for the South, the West, and the North. Close by folding your hands over your heart and extending this same goodness to yourself.

PRAYER

Teacher and Healer,
you brought the gift of yourself
to those who benefited from your work.
You touched them with wellsprings of love.
Remind me each day to do the same.
Consecrate all I do today
so my service to others brings a blessing.
I open the door of my heart to you.
I open the door.

I remind you to rekindle the gift of God that is within you . . . (2 Tm 1:6).

Week 6, Day 2

Bringing Love

The door of Room 204 became a literal barrier for an academic to shield his class and his students from harm. It stands as a reminder of the struggle and sacrifice. . . . On one side was a force of unblinking, unthinking hate. On the other side was a force of unbridled loyalty and, yes, love.

—Jonathan Turley

On April 16, 2007, the Virginia Tech massacre occurred in which a distraught student went on a shooting rampage, coldly killing fellow students. As many as fifteen were saved from death by an instinctively protective and caring English professor. Liviu Librescu pressed his body against the door to his classroom while he urged his students to jump out a window to safety. This professor, a Romanian Jew who survived the Nazis in his homeland years earlier, died in his classroom after the killer shot through the door that Librescu was holding shut.

Selfless love is real. In spite of the horrors of war and other brutal ways that humans treat one another, love is possible. Unselfish people reside everywhere. They love unconditionally, dedicate themselves to alleviating suffering, are willing to give their all for another, intent on being life-givers and spirit-transformers. These are not do-gooders, holier-than-thou people. No, this kind of love is seared by trials, purified by personal growth, shaped by persistent rededication and self-giving that goes beyond required duty. Each day people on this planet open the door of their hearts and love pours forth. No matter how discouraged we might get about the world's violence and hatred, let us remember that generous love thrives in kind souls and expresses itself daily.

Selfless love does not come about overnight. For most, it takes a lifetime of effort. Yet, nothing is more central to Christian life than other-centered love. "This is the first and last vocation of every Christian, to love, and all other vocations are only a shell in which this vocation, to love, is protected . . . ," writes Caryll Houselander. "Love, and love alone, can make life welcome to us; we can help one another by love, as never before; nothing else can comfort, encourage, be patient and heal, as love can do now."

Our deeds of love might not be as enormous as Liviu Librescu's, but they still contain great value. The unselfish giving and support we offer occurs within our homes and workplaces, in local supermarkets and on freeways, in hospitals, restaurants, and other common places of personal encounter. Dorothy Day, founder of the Catholic Worker movement, personified selfless love. She was convinced that each act of love had a far reaching effect: "If we all carry a little of the burden, it will be lightened. If we share in the suffering of the world, then some will not have to endure so heavy an affliction. . . . You may think you are alone. But we are all members of one another. We are children of God together."

At the conclusion of each day, the following inquiry of Evelyn Underhill's serves as a guide for reflection on the quality of our living: "Was everything that was done, done for love's sake? Were all the doors opened, that the warmth of Charity might fill the whole house; the windows cleaned, that they might more and more radiate from within its mysterious divine light?"

One of love's marvelous qualities is its capacity to never cease growing. As our selflessness expands, it continually affects our world. May a day never pass without attempting to keep in our hearts the expansive love that Brad and Jan Lundy visualize:

Imagine what life could be like if this love continued to expand, if it moved through our families, out into our neighborhoods and towns. Imagine waves of love continuing to roll, building in intensity, surging across boundaries and borders into other countries, dissolving barriers between people and nations. This Sea of Love grows in scope, in power, until everything in its path is absorbed by it, enlivened and healed by it. Until everything, everyone, is awash in Love. What will our world be like if Love is all there is?

Today, anoint the world with your love.

REFLECT ON THE FOLLOWING:
When have I experienced the selfless love of someone else? How have I shared selfless love with another?

MEDITATION
Enter into a contemplative spirit. Ease your body, mind, and heart. Recall the nearness of the Holy One and the immensity of this unreserved love. Read slowly several times the following verses from 1 Cor 13:4–8.

> Love is patient; love is kind;
> love is not envious or boastful
> or arrogant or rude.
> It does not insist on its own way;
> it is not irritable or resentful;
> it does not rejoice in wrongdoing,
> but rejoices in the truth. . . .
> Love never ends.

Sit quietly and let the qualities of love in this scripture passage deepen within you.

PRAYER
Everlasting Love,
within you resides all beneficence.
The generous love I receive from you

inspires and moves me to act unselfishly.
May the goodness dwelling within me
bless the lives of those I daily encounter.
Help me to share my love in spite of the cost.
I open the door of my heart to you.
I open the door.

Beloved, let us love one another, because love is from God (1 Jn 4:7).

WEEK 6, DAY 3

BRINGING RESPECT

I want to declare an open-door policy of the heart;
it gets wearisome scrutinizing everyone through
the peephole before sliding the deadbolt free.
—MARC IAN BARASCH

THE FURTHER WE enter our authentic self, the greater the contribution of our presence in the world. Within the confines of our inner sanctuary, fuller love arises and keener awareness grows of how intimately connected we are to all that exists. We become a nonjudgmental, listening, caring presence. Rather than engendering fear or animosity in us, the vast diversity of people with whom we engage enlarges our compassion and broadens our enthusiasm for the complex and mysterious nature of humanity.

As our world "grows smaller" through electronic communication and rapid travel, the locale in which we live increases in its assortment of individuals. The differences we bump into invite us to deliberately be a door of respectful presence. We open the door of our mind and heart to those persons whose ethnicity, religion, sexual orientation, and other personal traits and beliefs are opposed to, or different than, ours. By opening the door, we do not give up what we value and hold dear. Rather, our attitude is that of Christ: We look at a deeper level for what unites, instead of what divides. We approach each person with a sense of their innate blessedness.

This *seeing more deeply* is exemplified in a story by Adele Azar-Rucquoi in which she reflects on her volunteer work at a homeless shelter. Rucquoi tells how she gradually came to know the staff quite well and enjoyed their "wonderfully varied faith beliefs" until one man (whom she refers to as "B") made a statement completely contrary to what she believed. She felt sick to her stomach at the thought of what seemed to her a small, negative view that was quite the opposite of her vision regarding God's acceptance of every person. As Rucquoi struggled with B's comment for some weeks, she observed the man's behavior with the homeless. She noticed how gracious and nonjudgmental he was toward each one and concluded her reflection with this insight:

> Something happened inside me as we finished washing the last of the dirty pots. I looked up as if God were perched on a low rafter smiling. Oh, Lord, I get it. Sure, "B" may assert religious beliefs completely out of whack with my own. But "B" carries a heart grown bigger than his head. He is indeed a compassionate Christ, holding marginal people close in his heart. He treats them with dignity.

Rucquoi found her unity with "B" in their common desire to treat the homeless with compassion and kindness. We may have to search for quite a while, but we can usually find a thread that joins rather than separates us. We will never all be the same. This diversity is a gift, rather than a curse. As Mary Oliver explains, "If you are too much like myself, what shall I learn of you, or you of me?"

Diversity colors our world and keeps us from boxing ourselves into a tiny space with little room to breathe and expand. When we look with our inner eye, the one that God continually shines and clears, we see what is elusive but real: each person, regardless of how different they might be from us, has value and is worthy of our respect. Wayne Teasdale writes:

> We can only judge others if we can fulfill two conditions, that we know the other's heart totally, and that we love them unconditionally. Only God can possibly meet these two conditions, therefore only God can judge. Despite this truth, people continue to play God, and pass harsh and unfair judgments on others.

When the Corinthians were passing haughty judgments on one another, Saint Paul challenged them by using a metaphor of the human body to encourage respect and appreciation of their differences:

> If the foot would say, "Because I am not a hand, I do not belong to the body" that would not make it any less a part of the body. . . . The eye cannot say . . . "I have no need of you. . . ." If one member suffers, all suffer together with it; if one member is honored, all rejoice together with it. Now you are the body of Christ and individually members of it. (1 Cor 12:15–27)

Try to approach each person today with an inner eye that sees deeply.

Reflect on the following:

Think about the person, or group, that you have the most difficulty accepting. What is the deeper link that assists you in accepting your differences?

Meditation

Sit with palms up and open. Remember the indwelling presence of the Holy One. Pray for openness of mind and heart. Imagine you are sitting in a circle of three—yourself, the Holy One, and one person whom you dislike or find offensive. The three of you join hands in the circle. As you do so, divine love streams through each of you, filling you with a heartfelt awareness of the other person's core goodness. Stay with this connecting, flowing love until you sense a connection of oneness. Allow a movement of respect to enter and grow in your heart. Close with a prayer for peace and well-being.

PRAYER

> Creator of all that exists,
> your seeing is wide, deep, and clear.
> Turn me toward the unity I have with others.
> Touch my heart with your loving vision.
> Widen what is too narrow in my view.
> I want to value each person's innate worth.
> Help me appreciate the gift of diversity.
> I open the door of my heart to you.
> I open the door.

SCRIPTURE TO CARRY IN YOUR HEART TODAY:

Live in harmony with one another (Rom 15:5).

WEEK 6, DAY 4

BRINGING HOSPITALITY

To be fearless isn't really to overcome fear,
it's to come to know its nature.
Just open the door more and more
and at some point you'll feel capable of inviting
all sentient beings as your guests.
—PEMA CHÖDRÖN

IN MY TRAVELS to give retreats and conferences, I spend a lot of time in other peoples' physical space. I notice how I am met at the door. Usually I receive a glad welcome and generous hospitality. But sometimes people welcome me with their words and not their hearts. Apparently, I am an interruption or intrusion into their well-ordered, or well-scattered lives. My experience of being welcomed or unwelcomed encourages me to be alert to my own welcome of those in my life, whether for a short or a long period of time.

When I invited visitors to my website to send stories of their experiences regarding "doors," Marti Page sent an e-mail in which she described how an administrative assistant welcomed those who came to the door:

> My friend, Judy, worked in a parish office here in Massachusetts. As part of her job, she answered the front door, and would often be challenged by the person waiting for her on the other side. The windows around the door allowed her to see who was waiting for her. She often spoke about the three steps down she had to take before opening the door and of her desire to be Christ to whomever it was that was waiting for her to open the door.

How we welcome other human beings is how we welcome God. Jesus made this evident in his parable of separating the sheep from the goats. In this allegory, Jesus suggests a question that people will ask at the end of time: "And when was it that we saw you a stranger and welcomed you?" To which he replies, "Truly I tell you, just as you did it to one of the least of these who are members of my family, you did it to me" (Mt 25:31–40).

Think of the people in your life whom you welcome easily and those for whom you definitely need those "three steps down" to give you time to take a deep breath, to reorient your heart in order to greet them as another Christ. How often is your hospitality of heart challenged? What causes hesitation and reluctance when you take those "three steps down" to welcome those you dislike, or fear, or want to avoid?

There's a superb poem by Naomi Shihab Nye that reminds me of the times I've wavered in my hospitality, reluctant to open the door of my heart, only to discover the surprising gift awaiting me in the person I welcomed.

Nye refers to an old Arab adage that describes how to welcome strangers. This wise saying urges us to feed the strangers who come to our door for at least three days before ever asking anything about them, such as who they are, where they come from, or where they intend to go. Nye continues to develop this wise saying by noting that once the stranger has been fed, he or she will have enough strength to answer the questions. "Or," concludes Nye (with what I imagine is a twinkle in her eye) "By then you'll be/such good friends/you don't care."

I thought of this when I read a story about Denver Moore, the homeless man in *Same Kind of Different as Me*. Denver suffered a huge amount of life's harshness as a child, including being unable to save his beloved grandmother from burning to death in their rural cabin. Life became increasingly difficult for Denver and eventually he left what little he had to ride the trains as a hobo. The hostility that grew in his heart closed him off from everyone, even the two volunteers at a homeless shelter who gently reached out to him in his destitute and alienated condition. Only by approaching Denver with a genuine respect for who he was, did he slowly begin to trust. This welcoming love gradually opened the door of his heart, enabling him to bring forth the amazing wisdom dwelling inside. Like the Arab adage, the people at the shelter who befriended this stranger fed him for a long time before they found out anything about him. Eventually their patient kindness softened his deliberate distance and allowed a magnificent friendship to unfold.

The letter to the Hebrews advises: "Do not neglect to show hospitality to strangers, for by doing that some have entertained angels without knowing it" (Heb 13:2). "Strangers" are anyone outside the home of our heart whom we consider alien or foreign to our inner or outer space. While we ought not allow people to physically be part of our life if our bodily, mental, emotional, or spiritual safety is at risk, we cannot shun these people interiorly. Here we set aside estrangement, fear, and hostility and do our best to approach the "stranger" in spirit as one united with God and with us.

Do what you can to welcome the strangers who stand at the door of your heart today.

Reflect on the following:

What helps you, what hinders you, in welcoming "strangers" into your life?

Meditation

Rest your mind and heart. Be at ease with how you think and feel at this moment. Visualize yourself in a quiet spot where Christ is teaching. The crowd has dispersed and you are all alone with him now. Sit down together. Tell him about your experience of welcoming others. Then listen to the advice he gives you. Close your reflection by renewing your intention to be a person whose heart provides a loving reception for all its visitors.

Prayer

Divine Guest,
I lovingly welcome you
with the openness of my entire being.
I desire to receive people who are strangers
with this same spirit of graciousness.
Free my mind when it locks out others.
Disarm my heart of any armor it wears.
I open the door of my heart to you.
I open the door.

Scripture to carry in your heart today:

A certain woman named Lydia . . . urged us . . . "Come and stay at my home" (Acts 16:14–15).

BRINGING PEACE

If we have the will and determination
to mount such a peace offensive,
we will unlock hitherto tightly sealed doors of hope
and bring new light into the dark chambers of pessimism.
—MARTIN LUTHER KING, JR.

WHEN MARTIN LUTHER King, Jr. wrote the above words in 1967, he was referring to the nuclear arms race and the "discords of war." King was convinced that our energy ought to be focused on working for "peace and prosperity" for all nations, rather than on waging combat. While his words are fittingly directed toward massive wars between nations, his message applies equally to the warfare that goes on within the human heart and personal relationships.

I am convinced that peace among nations will not happen until there is true peace within the hearts of individuals. Within my own life a stronger peace has gradually taken root, mostly due to my commitment to daily, personal meditation. When I open the door of my heart and spend time with the Holy One, I become aware of what thwarts my effort to be peaceful. If I tend to the source of the distress, this, in turn, leads me to greater serenity. Then, when I move beyond the door of my heart into the wider world, this embraced peace accompanies me. Unless I deliberately choose to turn away from inner harmony, I can count on it to bless the people and the work of my life.

Becoming aware of my inner conflicts sometimes occasions a brutal recognition and uncompromising verdict of needing to change my ways. Learning about peace is one thing. Putting peace into practice by changing attitudes and actions is quite another. If unrest, nonforgiveness, dissension, apathy, or discontent reside in me, the scent of this will be on each breath I take. Discordance will contaminate each part of my life.

Here is what I suggest in order for peace to abide in our hearts and in our world:

- Place merciful peace on our lips when words of prejudice, gossip, shame, and blame are eager to be there.
- Draw forth humility from our heart when our ego seeks to triumph over and trounce the victims of our self-righteous superiority.
- Voice open, non-defensive dialogue when the loud anger and unfair accusations of others attempt to topple us with their ferocity.
- Work nonviolently for the active pursuit of peace when others opt for waging the aggression of war.
- Set to rest what screams for revenge. Bid farewell to what drains away kindness. Ease out old grudges, remnants of resentment, and any remainders of jealousy.
- Sift through the rubble of former battles with anyone. Sort out and discard the decomposed rot. Find what is salvageable. Save what benefits a growthful love.
- Resist attempts to mend what is beyond repair. Let go of what was but can be no more. Move on without reluctance or self-doubt.
- Free what trembles with fear. Embrace what longs for acceptance. Forego anxiety and worry, which steal peace from the soul and add to inner turbulence.
- Resist the desire to grasp. Have only what is essential for life.

Today, bring peace with you to every creature, to solitary corners and crowded streets, to each hostility and every anxiety. Most of all, embrace confidently the bountiful peace of Indwelling Love so your presence in the world becomes one of healing tranquility.

Reflect on the following:

Does something need to change within your heart and life in order for you to bring more peace into the world?

MEDITATION

Begin by going within to where the Holy One is the deep source of your serenity. Sense an easy flowing peace moving through your body and soul. Open the door of your heart and let this peace move outward to wherever you will be today. Visualize tranquility emitting from the pores of your body, mind, and spirit. Notice how this peace stretches beyond you and permeates all it touches. Return now to your heart-space. Remain in the serene awareness of God's presence until it is time for you to close your prayer. Go forth to make a difference in the world.

PRAYER

Divine Peace-Bringer,
take what is jagged in my relationships
and transform it with your grace.
I will do my best to bid farewell
to whatever keeps me from inner peace.
Help me bring your enduring harmony
into every part of my existence.
I open the door of my heart to you.
I open the door.

SCRIPTURE TO CARRY IN YOUR HEART TODAY:

Do not let your hearts be troubled (Jn 14:1).

WEEK 6, DAY 6

BRINGING HOPE

Approach this new door
with great confidence in your heart,
for you have so much to offer.
Open each new door with trust,
holding your dreams very near . . .
knowing the world is waiting
for the goodness and the love you carry within you.
—M. E. MIRO

A FEW WEEKS before Easter, I returned from leading a Lenten retreat in Ohio where I spoke about the urgency of keeping a hope-filled heart amid our personal travails and the world's violent disturbances. Soon after this, I received a letter from Meg, one of the retreatants. She told me that a week after the retreat she found a small bird's nest built in a wreath she had placed on the family's front door. A few days after that, Meg noticed three eggs in the nest. She and her family were "waiting anxiously to see when and if the eggs would hatch."

Meg went on to tell me how she was immersed in spring, in Lent, and the journey toward Easter. She saw the nest symbolizing hope. A month later Meg wrote to tell me that five healthy baby finches hatched, developed quickly, outgrew the nest, and flew away, all in the space of that short time. Hope is, indeed, like a nest holding tiny eggs. The difference is that our unrealized dreams usually take much longer to hatch and grow wings.

Each opening of the door to our heart provides an opportunity to strengthen our hope. Each journey inward allows restoration of the belief that we can know our inherent goodness, birth it into being, and not give up on the possibility of our innate love to outgrow egocentricity and overt disregard for others.

The hope we bring with us from our prayer and reflection consists of numerous expressions, but some commonalities serve as a central foundation on which we can build our hope. These include the following:

- Our ability to live what we believe is the heart of our spiritual identity.
- Our intrinsic goodness can contribute to the world's transformation.
- Something of benefit eventually evolves from our daily dyings.
- An eternal Presence companions us with unwavering fidelity.
- We are emissaries of hope when we give our focus to the present moment rather than to regrets of the past or concerns about the future.

Hope does not cause us to run from what we experience or to deny it. Rather, it gives us a reason to embrace what we experience and go forward with assurance. When I was in the throes of grief, I had a night dream that kept me believing my sorrow would pass. In the dream, I was in the basement of my house. The walls were made of earthen clay with big stones protruding from them. On each stone was written one word: "Alleluia!" I awoke with a smile, assured that my joy was as durable as the stones in my dream and would not die.

Having hope does not mean everything will turn out the way we want. Vandana Shiva, the gifted scientist and environmentalist from India, often faces great obstacles to her work. She was asked, "What keeps you so alive?" She replied:

> I do not allow myself to be overcome by hopelessness, no matter how tough the situation . . . if you just do your little bit without thinking of the bigness of what you stand against, if you turn to the enlargement of your own capacities, just that in itself creates new potential. And I've learned . . . to detach myself from the results of what I do, because those are not in my hands. The context is not in your control, but your commitment is yours to make, and you can make the deepest commitment with a total detachment about where it will take you. You want it to lead to a better world, and you

shape your actions and take full responsibility for them, but then you have detachment. And that combination of deep passion and deep detachment allows me to always take on the next challenge because I don't cripple myself, I don't tie myself in knots. . . . I think what we owe each other is a celebration of life and to replace fear and hopelessness with fearlessness and joy.

Celebrate life today. Take hope with you in all you are and all you do.

REFLECT ON THE FOLLOWING:

What is the hope you carry with you into the world?

MEDITATION

Go to an open doorway. Stand in it facing east, the place of the rising sun, the direction of hope. Raise your arms. Move them around you in the doorway. Feel the open space, the lack of a barrier to your ability to move freely. Continue standing (or sit) in the doorway. Breathing in, receive the love of your divine companion. Accept the fresh vitality of this enduring presence. Breathing out, lovingly send this presence as a gift of hope to all that exists. Conclude your meditation by forming a brief statement for how you will be a presence of hope wherever you go.

PRAYER

Heart of Hope,
you draw me to hear the world's heartache.
You strengthen my spirit when I feel frail.
You encourage me when I am disheartened.
You enliven me when I sense helpless rigidity.
I go now to share what you daily give to me.
Thank you that I can be your channel of hope.
Once again, I open the door of my heart to you.
I open the door.

Scripture to carry in your heart today:

Now hope that is seen is not hope. For who hopes for what is seen? But if we hope for what we do not see, we wait for it with patience (Rom 8:24–25).

Week 6, Day 7

Review and Rest

This is your day to gather what has taken place for you during the past week of using this book. It is also meant to be a day of rest for you. Let this reflection and integration time be a gentle pause in your week.

Begin

"A Prayer for Openness" (page 13).

Review

Look back over the week. If you wrote in your journal, review what you've written. If you did not write, sit quietly for a few minutes and let your reflections from this week visit you. Then, respond in writing to the following:

1. The most helpful part of the past week's reflection and prayer was . . .
2. The most challenging part of the past week's reflection and prayer was . . .
3. I want to remember . . .
4. I hope that . . .
5. I wonder . . .

Complete your reflection with a one- or two-line summary of your experience from the week. An alternative to writing might be to summarize the week by drawing, sculpting, creating music, dancing, or using some other form of alternative expression to gather and integrate the week's experience into your present situation.

Another alternative to writing would be to summarize each week by drawing a door. Place words, phrases, drawings, or other symbols on the door to depict what happened within the week to draw you into further growth. (Instead of drawing a door, you could post these words, etc., on a real door in your home.)

CONCLUDE

Close with one of the prayers from the week and/or by sitting quietly for a few minutes of gratitude.

AS YOU GO FORTH

See what I mean? Take one small thing in hand,
open it up, and there's another door,
and another, long corridors of views
into the heart of darkness and light.
There's no such thing as a small portion
once you bite in and savor the flavors.
—JULIA ALVAREZ

DURING THE PAST six weeks you have engaged in an ever deepening process of opening the door to your true self. The last page has been turned. Here you are. As I conclude this book, I wonder what you will be experiencing. Relief at completion? Courage to go forward? Satisfaction at insights gained? Sadness at the culmination? Allurement toward further exploration and growth? I hope the latter response remains uppermost in your mind and heart.

When you chose to move through *Open the Door,* you stepped into one segment of a lifetime of exploration. These six weeks compose only one small part of discovering your genuine self. Julia Alvarez gets it right in the above section of her poem "Small Portions." Open one door and there's another and another. Alvarez perceives the process of growth clearly: we live our journey through the small pieces of life that we experience each day. As you go on with your life, other inner doors will become visible. You will continue to hear the knock of the Holy One and find yourself on yet another threshold. As you repeatedly grow in acceptance of your goodness, its spiritual abundance will accompany you into the marketplace.

Alvarez's insight reminds me of an artist friend's comment after she visited an ancient Indian pueblo in New Mexico's Chaco Canyon. Kristy marveled at what she found. Through an open doorway leading into one of the dwellings, she looked inside and saw another doorway to a room beyond it. Radiant light streamed through the doorway leading to the additional rooms. The beckoning illumination held the power of drawing her further into the dwelling where open space abounded. After Kristy described this to me, she mused with soft amazement in her voice, "Is this what heaven, nirvana, enlightenment is like—that nothing closes us out, nothing stands in our way?"

The Light on our path of life draws us beyond where we now are. We continue to open the door of our heart until nothing stands in the way of our true self's complete expression of love. Each turning inward, each expansion of our authenticity, each strengthening connection with the divine, brings us more fully into this "heaven." Each movement of the heart leads us closer to the moment when all becomes one, when there are no more doors, only an all-encompassing, light-filled realm of peace in which we experience an Ancient Love forever drawing us into communion.

As you travel beyond these pages, you may wonder about the benefits of this six-week journey. You may not have definite proof of this, but I firmly believe your inner journey brings with it untold blessings for both yourself and others. None of us know when or how opening the door of our heart might make a difference to those nearby or to those in the larger global story of transformation.

As I have noted throughout this book, the external opening of doors symbolizes what happens internally. Such is the situation of a man named Dan who chose to return to the city of his birth. As he visited his childhood neighborhood, Dan felt a deep yearning to go inside the home where he lived as a young boy. In spite of hesitations and a fear of not being welcomed, he went to his old house of over sixty years earlier and knocked on the door. The woman living there opened the door a tiny crack and asked him cautiously what he wanted. Once Dan explained his motivation, she opened the door and welcomed him inside. She called her husband and together they took their visitor through the entire house with its precious memories. With a full heart, Dan prepared to depart. When he expressed his gratitude, the gracious woman responded, "I have been wanting for a long time to visit the home of my childhood. You have given me the courage to do it."

Had Dan not knocked on the door of his home place and had the woman not opened the door to him, nothing more would have transpired. As it is, one person's courage freed the other's. When we open the door to our heart, we enable others to release their own.

Thank you for wholeheartedly entering into the past six weeks, for not giving up on the difficult days, for trusting the deepest part of who you are, for returning again and again to the work required even when finding time to do so challenged your full schedule. You have discovered and claimed more of your authentic self. You know now that the process of accepting and sharing your innate goodness is the process of a lifetime. Go forward with hope.

Rituals for Groups to Integrate/ Celebrate Each Week

Upon completion of the first draft of this book, I invited a group of five women and three men to experience the manuscript by reading and praying with its contents. We met every Tuesday evening for six weeks to discuss their reflection and prayer. The suggestions for group gatherings in this appendix are similar to the questions and prayers we used for those gatherings. Here are a few notes about the Group Gatherings.

Be creative

Please feel free to adapt the ideas I offer for each week. Add or delete items and processes according to your own inspiration and the group's approach to spirituality. What I am providing is a basic structure on which you can build.

Music

The songs I suggest for use come from the sources listed at the end of this introduction.

Group sharing

The gatherings are structured for a timeframe of about one-and-a-half hours. If the group consists of more than five participants, it is best to move into smaller groups of three to five persons when responding to the questions. This allows adequate time for each one to share with greater depth and quality.

Unless your group has been together for a long time, go over some basic rules for faith sharing:

- Each one responds to a specific question before anyone else speaks a second time.
- The focus is on attentive and compassionate listening.
- The gathering is not about trying to solve anyone's difficulties.
- Encourage participants to be aware of their talking too much or too little.
- Each one is, of course, free to "pass" by not sharing on a particular topic or question.

What is revealed in the small group remains confidential. When re-gathering for the larger group with general responses, permission of the person is needed before sharing any quotes or specific content that this participant shared in the smaller group.

RESOURCES FOR MUSIC

Awakening Consciousness, Jan Novotka. www.jannovotka.com

I Open to You: Chants, composed by Joyce Rupp, sung by Marlene Fitzpatrick, Kim Schroeder, Linda Yagel. Notre Dame, IN: Ave Maria Press. www.avemariapress.com

In the Name of All That Is, Jan Novotka. www.jannovotka.com

Morning Light, Saint Louis Jesuits. Portland, OR: OCP Publications. www.ocp.org

O Healing Light of Christ, Carey Landry. Portland, OR: OCP Publications. www.ocp.org

Out of the Ordinary: Chants, composed by Joyce Rupp, sung by Bridget Pasker. Notre Dame, IN: Ave Maria Press. www.avemariapress.com

Seven Sacred Pauses, Velma Frye. www.velmafrye.com

A Special Collection, Monica Brown. www.emmausproductions.com

We Will Remember, Carmel Boyle. www.ancroi.iej, www.ancroi@aircom.net

Most of the musical notation for *I Open to You* is in *Dear Heart, Come Home*. Musical notation for *Out of the Ordinary* is in the book with the same title.

Week 1

Process and Prayer

Greeting One Another

The leader welcomes the participants and invites them to focus on their inner treasure. They close their eyes and place their hands over their hearts. Then they repeat the following scripture verse after the leader:

Do you not know that you are God's temple
and that God's Spirit dwells in you? (1 Cor 3:16)

After this, they stand and find one other person whom they face. The participants are asked to gaze directly into the eyes of the other person as they repeat the scripture verse after the leader, addressing its message to the person across from them.

The group now forms a circle. They say the verse together several times while looking at one another in the circle.

Chant

"In God We Live," CD: *I Open to You*. (If using the CD, the word "God" is changed to "You" in order to address the divine more personally.)

In You we live and move. In You we have our being.
In You we shall remain. In You is our abiding.

PRAYER *(together)*

Divine Companion, we gather to share with one another what you have stirred in our hearts. As we do so, our openness to one another reflects your welcoming way with each of us. Help us listen attentively to one another. Deepen our sense of your presence among us. Strengthen our desire to be spiritually transformed. Amen.

SMALL-GROUP DIALOGUE

Offer any general comments on your experience of this week's reflection and prayer.

In what way has God been a door for you?

What kind of door symbolizes who you are now? (If you drew or painted a door during the week, feel free to share this.)

Who has especially helped you open the door to your deeper self? How did this happen?

Which question of the week especially tugged at your mind or heart?

Is there anything else from the week that you would like to share with the group?

LARGE-GROUP SHARING

What did you discover and experience in listening to others in your group?

What are some aspects from this week's prayer and reflection that you want to remember and deepen in your life?

PRAYER TO THE ONE WHO IS THE DOOR

Response to each of the following: We welcome you, Door to the Sacred.

You stand at the door of our hearts and offer us the joy of your constant companionship . . .

You stand at the door of our heart and offer us merciful forgiveness for our failings . . .

You stand at the door of our heart and offer us the ability to welcome more of our authentic self...

You stand at the door of our heart and offer us inherent wisdom to guide our way...

You stand at the door of our heart and offer us strength to walk with our struggles...

You stand at the door of our heart and offer us unconditional love...

You stand at the door of our heart and offer us the gift of mystery...

You stand at the door of our heart and call us to go inward to the unknown and the unnamed, to seek our home in you...

The Leader invites participants to add their own "You stand at the door of our hearts and offer us. . . ." Then all pray together.

God-with-us, you are the Door to our true self. Lead and direct us to doors that need opening. Motivate and challenge us to receive those whose lives ask for our openness and love. Thank you for standing at the door of our hearts and waiting for us to give you a welcome. As we turn inward to the door of our deepest self, we trust that you are our companion and guide. Amen.

SONG

"O Beauty, Ever Ancient," Saint Louis Jesuits (CD: *Morning Light*) or "Touch My Life," Monica Brown (CD: *A Special Collection*) or a similar song acknowledging our longing for the divine and affirming the beauty of our soul.

BLESSING

Stand in a circle. Each one speaks her or his name aloud. The whole group turns toward that person, calling by name: "_____, go through the doors of change with confidence in God and in yourself."

WEEK 2

PROCESS AND PRAYER

The song "Standing at the Door" can be sung as a whole group, or the participants can form two groups. [This song is not on a CD but the musical notation is in the back of the book, Out of the Ordinary.*] With two groups, one side faces the other and sings the first two lines to them. The second group responds by singing the next two lines back to them. After singing the lines a few times, the second group sings the first two lines and the first group responds with the second two lines.*

> Standing at the door. Standing at the door.
> Will you open to me? Will you open to me?
> I will open to you. I will open to you.
> Standing at the door. I will open to you.*

SONG
"My Soul's Desire," Carmel Boyle (*We Will Remember*) or the chant, "Here I Am" (*Out of the Ordinary: Chants*).

PRAYER *(together)*
Loving Guide, you stand at the door of our lives, always available to us. Thank you for inspiring and encouraging us to knock on the door of our hearts. May we be aware of your presence in each one who gathers here. Open our minds and hearts as we listen to one another's story of growth. Amen.

Small-Group Dialogue

Offer any general comments on your experience of this week's reflection and prayer.

What is your experience of listening to the Holy One's knock on your door of life?

Choose any two of the following questions from Carmel Boyle's song and share your response with the group.

> What is your hope? What is your song?
> What is your hurt? What is your joy?
> What is your wisdom? What is your fire?

What is the message you would like to slip under the door to God?

What message do you think God would slip under your door?

Which question of the week especially tugged at your mind or heart?

Is there anything else from the week that you would like to share with the group?

Large-Group Sharing

What did you discover and experience in listening to others in your group?

What are some aspects from this week's prayer and reflection that you want to remember and deepen in your life?

Standing Before the Door

Visualize yourself standing before a door.

The Holy One is on the other side and knocks.

See yourself opening the door. . . .

Welcome the Holy One into your life once again . . . (*pause*).

Sing: I will open to you. . . .

Standing at the door. I will open to you.

See yourself once more standing before a door.

Your self, with your strengths and limitations,

waits on the other side and knocks. . . .

Place your hand in the hand of the Holy One.
Open the door and welcome your self . . . (*pause*).
Sing: I will open to you. . . .

Bring to mind a loved one you want to be united with today.
Picture that person standing at the door of your heart, knocking. . . .
Place your hand in the hand of the Holy One.
Welcome this person into your heart of love . . . (*pause*).
Sing: I will open to you. . . .

Visualize the person you have the most trouble with in your life.
This person is standing at the door of your heart, awaiting an entrance. . . .
Place your hand in the hand of the Holy One.
Open the door at least a little bit further than you have in the past.
See if you can welcome this person into your heart . . . (*pause*).
Sing: I will open to you. . . .

Once more you are standing before a door.
Picture at this door a group of people in our world
who struggle with life-and-death issues.
They stand there awaiting your compassionate welcome. . . .
Again, join hands with the Holy One and invite these people to come
into your heart. . . .

PRAYER (*together or by the leader*)
Remind us often, compassionate and welcoming God, that those who
stand at the door of our hearts awaiting an entrance bear your image and
likeness. May we be open, loving, and gracious human beings. Amen.

BLESSING
Offer a gesture of peace to one another.

Week 3

Process and Prayer

Greeting One Another

Approach each one in the group. For every person you greet, hold your hands over your heart. Open your hands outward toward the person before you as you address him or her by name: "____, I open my heart to you." Bow gently and move on to the next person.

Reading

The door to my heart broke open.
At last You Yourself stood there.
My heart drifted toward You
on a stream of tears.
Then it rejoiced at Your feet.
From the heavens the light of dawn
held out its arms to me.
At the broken door of my prison
the victory cries filled the air. Hurrah!

—Rabindranath Tagore

Chant

"O, I Open to You" (CD: *I Open to You*).

Prayer *(together)*

Door of Life, open our hearts to one another as we gather to reflect on our journey with you. Free us from any resistance we might have to sharing what you have given us in our prayer and meditation. Thank you for the gift each one brings to this time and place. Stir within us an ever deepening desire to be our truest self. Amen.

SMALL-GROUP DIALOGUE

Offer any general comments on your experience of this week's reflection and prayer.

Which kind of "oil for the hinges" does your life need at this time?

Did you think of other "oils" besides the ones listed in Day Two?

Share a life experience in which openness played a vital part for your growth.

How do you relate to the unwanted aspects of your self?

Which question of the week especially tugged at your mind or heart?

Is there anything else from the week that you would like to share with the group?

LARGE-GROUP SHARING

What did you discover and experience in listening to others in your group?

What are some aspects from this week's prayer and reflection that you want to remember and deepen in your life?

SONG

Listen to or sing: "The Truth," Velma Frye (CD: *Seven Sacred Pauses*).

PRAYER

Respond to each line on the following page with these words:

One and only companion,
my Beloved!
Behold! My door lies
open and inviting.

—RABINDRANATH TAGORE

The abundance of the Holy One's unconditional love dwells in us ...
The ability to be compassionate and nonjudgmental dwells in us ...
The strength to unlock the door of our heart dwells in us ...
The power to forgive our self and forgive others dwells in us ...
The spirit of nonviolence and peace-making dwells in us ...
The selflessness to reach beyond our tightly held ego-interests dwells in us ...
The capacity to be filled with ongoing gratitude dwells in us ...
The adventurous energy of continual growth dwells in us ...
The courage of going deeper into our hidden well of wisdom dwells in us ...
The faithfulness of being ever more fully in union with God dwells in us ...

MAKING A COMMITMENT TO BE OPEN TO GROWTH

Each participant stands in an open doorway, one at a time. Standing in the doorway, each one proclaims:

I will be open to who I am and who I can become.

All respond to the person standing in the doorway with this blessing:

May your heart be opened a little further every day.

After all have stood in the open doorway and made their commitment, close with everyone standing in a circle, joining hands, and singing the chant "O, I Open to You" several times.

WEEK 4

PROCESS AND PRAYER

GREETING ONE ANOTHER

As a symbol of the mystery and silent waiting of the threshold experience, each one makes a silent bow to another, honoring the Holy One's indwelling presence. Greet each person in the group in this manner.

READINGS

1. There is a breath of warmth, compassion, and creativity that comes from inside, from the darkness, from the womb of all beings. According to the Native Middle Eastern tradition, the womb reality was present at the beginning, preparing for the primeval fire-ball. In this process of birth, some part of individuality is sacrificed and cleansed with each new creation. This womb reality is available in our bodies and our collective psyche both as the fear of darkness and as a power of rejuvenation.

—*Desert Wisdom,* Neil Douglas-Klotz

2. When Pharaoh let the people go, God did not lead them by way of the land of the Philistines, although that was nearer; for God thought, "If the people face war, they may change their minds and return to Egypt." So God led the people by the roundabout way of the wilderness toward the Red Sea.

—Exodus 13:17–18

3. Very truly, I tell you, unless a grain of wheat falls into the earth and dies, it remains just a single grain; but if it dies, it bears much fruit.

—John 12:24

CHANT

"Passing Over" (CD: *I Open to You)* or "Well of Silence" (*Awakening Consciousness,* Jan Novotka).

PRAYER *(together)*

Womb of Love, time and again, we wait on the threshold for you to nurture us in our spiritual gestation. Once more, we open our minds and hearts, trusting that you are present with us and among us. With courage and confidence we gather here, ready to share our journey with one another. Thank you for being with us. Amen.

SMALL-GROUP DIALOGUE

Offer any general comments on your experience of this week's reflection and prayer.

What aspect of "the threshold" most challenges you . . . letting go, darkness, liminality, waiting, making choices, etc.?

What threshold situation particularly influenced your life? How did this happen?

How have you experienced "the gargoyles" and "the guardians" of your spiritual journey?

Which question of the week especially tugged at your mind or heart?

Is there anything else from the week that you would like to share with the group?

LARGE-GROUP SHARING

What did you discover and experience in listening to others in your group?

What are some aspects from this week's prayer and reflection that you want to remember and deepen in your life?

SONG

Listen to "Be Still," Carey Landry (CD: *O Healing Light of Christ*) or "Be Still," Carmel Boyle *(CD: We Will Remember)*.

COMMITMENT TO STAND ON THE THRESHOLD OF LIFE IN ORDER TO GROW

If possible, turn out all lights in the room except one small candle, just enough light to find one's way to the open doorway. The group stands in silence while each participant takes a turn at standing on the threshold of the door. Once on the threshold, the person proclaims: "I believe I can grow in the darkness" *(or words of one's own choosing). The leader then rings a bell after each proclamation to announce the "new life" of transformation gestating in the darkness.*

PRAYER *(together)*

> God of the threshold
> this we pray:
> that what comes in
> enters by consent,
> by invitation
> that what passes through
> crosses over with grace,
> with mercy
> that what dwells within
> resides in delight,
> in integrity
> that what goes forth
> emerges for peace,
> for blessing.

Offer a sign of peace to one another.

WEEK 5

PROCESS AND PRAYER

GREETING ONE ANOTHER
Each participant approaches another with a bow and with the follow-ing words: "I greet the power of transformation in you." *Move around the group and greet each person.*

CHANT
"We Are Moving On" (CD: *Out of the Ordinary: Chants*).

BODY PRAYER
This is led by the facilitator who invites participants to place their hands near the particular part of the body being acknowledged. Pause briefly after each statement before continuing on to the next one.

Placing hands over the eyes:
Let us resolve to change the way we look at ourselves, others, life, God, and to move on from false ways of seeing.

Placing hands over the ears:
Let us resolve to close the ears of our inner self to voices telling us we are less than we are meant to be.

Placing hands over the mouth:
Let us resolve to close our mouth in order to keep from speaking words and giving messages that do not reflect our authentic self.

Placing hands over the forehead:
Let us close our inner door to ideas and attitudes, to old memories and hurts, to all that holds us back from growth.

Placing hands over the heart:

We remember the door of our heart. Let us resolve to leave behind whatever keeps us from being persons of loving kindness, to move toward what will benefit not only ourselves but all creation.

SMALL-GROUP DIALOGUE

Offer any general comments on your experience of this week's reflection and prayer.

Which prerequisites for closing the door listed in the introduction do you find most helpful?

Were there others that could be added?

What life-experience led you to close a door that brought about growth for you?

What thoughts and feelings stir when you think about your own "exit door"?

Which question of the week especially tugged at your mind or heart?

Is there anything else from the week that you would like to share with the group?

LARGE-GROUP SHARING

What did you discover and experience in listening to others in your group?

What are some aspects from this week's prayer and reflection that you want to remember and deepen in your life?

PAUSE FOR QUIET

Reflect on the door of your life that needs closing; renew your desire to put behind you that which distracts or denies you the ability to move into fuller growth.

PRAYER *(prayed in silence)*

Remove from me anything that leads me to believe less, to hope less, to love less. I am willing to do whatever on my part needs to be done. If you are using any defect to help me become more believing, more helpful, more loving, I am willing to keep it, trusting in your love. Help me to live in awareness and be faithful to the struggle.

—BARBARA BREAUD

MAKING A COMMITMENT TO CLOSE THE DOOR

Write on a small piece of paper (using a symbol or a code) what you need to leave behind in order to move on. Participants come, one at a time, to a bowl that has been placed on a table. Tear the paper into pieces. Drop the pieces in the bowl. After all have done this, the leader takes the bowl out of the room to dispose of the papers, being sure to close the door completely as the bowl is taken away. The group sits silently until the leader returns.

PRAYER

One person reads the scripture verse and the entire group joins in the prayer.

Come, my people, enter your chambers, and shut your doors behind you; hide yourselves for a little while until the wrath is past (Is 26:20).

> May I have the wisdom to know when to close the door, when to separate myself from the "wrath" of whatever keeps me from pureness of mind and heart.

If any want to become my followers, let them deny themselves and take up their cross daily and follow me. For those who want to save their life will lose it, and those who lose their life for my sake will save it (Lk 9:23–24).

> May I recognize the unhealthy ego and the false self. May I draw forth the courage to "lose my life" in order to find it more fully in the heart of God.

When they had brought their boats to shore, they left everything and followed Jesus (Lk 5:11).

May I respond to the call of the Holy One in each part of my life. May I be willing to follow this loving voice, and close the door to what keeps me from dedication to the Great Teacher.

Jesus would withdraw to deserted places and pray (Lk 5:16).

May I know when it is time to withdraw from life's activities, to seek solitude and intentional time with my Inner Source of goodness.

Very truly, I tell you, unless the grain of wheat falls into the earth and dies, it remains just a single grain; but if it dies, it bears much fruit (Jn 12:24).

May I yield to the deep journey of surrender and have confidence that the door I close behind me will open to new life.

Know that I am with you and will keep you wherever you go (Gn 28:15).

May I trust the sheltering wings of the divine to surround and protect me when I take the fearful step of closing the door behind me.

When (Paul) had finished speaking, he knelt down with them all and prayed. There was much weeping among them all; they embraced Paul and kissed him, grieving especially because of what he had said, that they would not see him again (Acts 20:36–38).

May I approach my exit door of death with a strong belief that there is more beyond the finality and completion of bodily existence.

Close with offering a sign of peace to one another.

Week 6

Prayer and Process

Reading

Every sound
has a home
from which it has come
to us
and a door
through which it is going
again,
out into the world
to make another home.

— David Whyte

Greeting One Another

Participants sit quietly for a moment after they are invited to think about what quality of their inner world they want to resound in the external world. They then arise and greet each person with this quality. They do so in this manner: holding out both hands, palms up, extended toward the other person, saying "I bring you the gift of _____." Make a gentle bow toward that person and go on to the next.

Chant

"All of My Life" (CD: *Out of the Ordinary: Chants*).

Four Directions Prayer

Face each of the directions as the facilitator reads the first section and all respond. Pause for a moment after extending your goodness before turning to the next direction.

East

We open the door of our heart to the East, the bearer of dawn, the place of hope. We remember those whose dreams have died, whose hearts have lost hope, those who suffer in the shadows of neglect and abuse. Let us send our love to all in the East.

All: I extend the goodness dwelling within me to all in the East.

South

We open the door of our heart to the South, where intense sunlight grows and nourishes the fecundity of earth. We remember there are many whose inner gardens feel barren, whose lives are emptied of the basic necessities of life. We compassionate earth and sea whose vibrant substance has been damaged by human disregard. Let us send our love to all in the South.

All: I extend the goodness dwelling within me to all in the South.

West

We open the door of our heart to the West, where the sun sets and night follows. We remember those who face life-changing transitions, whose physical, mental, or emotional security is being challenged, those who are falling into the darkness of depression or despair. Let us send our love to all in the West.

All: I extend the goodness dwelling within me to all in the West.

North

We open the door of our heart to the North, where ancient stones of durability and glaciers of calmness stand in silent repose. We remember those who are caught in the terrors of war, those who are victims of violence, all whose lives cry out for the stability and calmness of peace. Let us send our love to all in the North.

All: I extend the goodness dwelling within me to all in the North.

Stand in a circle. Silently extend goodness to one another. Then pray together:

May all I do each day be for the healing of the whole.
May all I do each day mend our broken world.
May all I do each day bring blessings on the Earth.
May all I do each day be for the good of all.
All I do each day.

—JAN NOVATKA

SMALL-GROUP DIALOGUE

Offer any general comments on your experience of this week's reflection and prayer.

With which theme of the week did you most easily relate? Was any theme difficult for you?

What motivates you to move from the inner door of your heart and go beyond into the external sphere of life? What holds you back from doing this?

What is the hope you want to bring with you into the world?

Which question of the week especially tugged at your mind or heart?

How have these six weeks you have shared together influenced your journey of life?

LARGE-GROUP SHARING

What did you discover and experience in listening to others in your group?

What are some aspects from this week's prayer and reflection that you want to remember and deepen in your life?

Song

"The Presence You Are," Jan Novotka (CD: *Awakening to Consciousness*).
It's not what you do, but how you do it.
It's not what you see, but how you see.
It's not what you say, what you know or achieve.
But it's the presence, the presence you are.

Prayer

Pray in alternate sides, with everyone praying the last two lines of the blessing.

May the door of my inner home be wide enough
to receive those who hunger for kindness,
those who are lonely, or isolated from friendship.
May it welcome those who have cares to unburden,
thanks to express, hopes to nurture.
May the door of my heart be narrow enough
to shut out pettiness and pride, envy and enmity.
May the door of my heart be closed to self-righteousness,
selfishness, and harshness.
May its threshold be no stumbling block
to receiving those who are different than I am.

All: May my inner home be for all who enter,
the doorway to spiritual richness and a more meaningful life.

—THE SIDDUR OF SHIR CHADASH

Blessing

This is done in partners. The facilitator speaks the blessing while the participants look directly at one another, placing their hands near the part of the body that is being blessed. The only words the participants speak are the last three lines.

Forehead

May the door of your mind be open. May you seek to resolve anything in your thoughts and attitudes that keeps you from being your authentic self.

Ears

As you stand daily at the door of your life, may you listen to the voice of the Holy One and heed the direction to which this beloved presence beckons you.

Eyes

May the door of your eyes be open. May you look for and recognize your own goodness, as well as the goodness of each person you meet along the road of life.

Mouth

When you open the door of your mouth, may you find the courage to voice with loving integrity what is truest within you.

Feet

When you stand on the threshold of your inner life, may you do so with patient hope, believing that gestation is occurring during those foggy times of searching and waiting.

Hands

As each of your inward journeys prepares you to enter the external world, may you stretch forth your hands in compassionate service.

Heart

As you journey onward, may the door of your heart continually swing open so that you keep growing in union with the Eternal Source of Love.

The facilitator invites the participants to repeat each of the following lines.

Whisper in the other person's ear:

"Continue to open the door of your heart."
"Open it as fully as you can."
"Be at peace."

Notes

Introduction

Authors employ the word "self" in a variety of ways. In this book, references to "self" represent the essential nature of a person. The self includes both the authentic or true aspect of one's being, as well as the inauthentic or false dimension. Thus, I refer to "our self" rather than to "our selves" when using this term. The same applies to the use of the word "heart" when it pertains to our nonphysical being.

de Waal, Esther. *Lost in Wonder: Rediscovering the Spiritual Art of Attentiveness* (Norwich, Norfolk: Canterbury Press, 2003), 24.

Pierre Teilhard de Chardin, Writings selected and introduced by Ursula King (Maryknoll, NY: Orbis Books, 1999), 50.

Merton, Thomas. *New Seeds of Contemplation* (New York: New Directions Publishing Corporation, 2007), 61.

Bruteau, Beatrice. *What We Can Learn From the East* (New York: Crossroad Publishing Company, 1995), 53. Titled "Christ at Heart's Door," this image can be seen at www.anderson.edu/sallman/heartsdoor.html

Tagore, Rabindranath. *Gitanjali* (Jacksonville, FL: Filiquarian Publishing, 2007), #101, 113.

Week 1

Introduction

Wiederkehr, Macrina. *The Song of the Seed: The Monastic Way of Tending the Soul* (San Francisco: HarperSanFrancisco, 1995), 113.

Kunitz, Stanley and Genine Lentine. *The Wild Braid: A Poet Reflects on a Century in the Garden* (New York: W.W. Norton & Co., 2007), 87.

Day 1

Winterson, Jeanette. *Lighthousekeeping* (New York: Harcourt, Inc., 2004), 218–219.

Day 2

Both the *Book of Exodus* and the *Book of Numbers* in the Jewish scriptures describe the wilderness journey of the Israelites.

Day 3

Leder, Drew. *Sparks of the Divine* (Notre Dame, IN: Sorin Books, 2004), 106.

Markova, Dawna. *I Will Not Die an Unlived Life: Reclaiming Purpose and Passion* (York Beach, ME: Conari Press, 2000), 33.

Wicks, Robert J. *Crossing the Desert: Learning to Let Go, Live Simply, and See Clearly* (Notre Dame, IN: Sorin Books, 2007), 151–152.

Markova, 33.

Day 4

Lamott, Anne. *Grace (Eventually): Thoughts on Faith* (New York: River-head Books, 2007), 107.

Ohanneson, Joan. *Scarlet Music: Hildegard of Bingen: A Novel* (New York: Crossroad Publishing Company, 1997), 193.

Davies, David. "Book Bites," *Faith at Work* (Summer, 2007): 28.

Week 2

Introduction

de Waal, 11.

This reflection is from the monthly booklet, *Living With Christ,* July 2005.

Day 1

Hanh, Thich Nhat. "The Teaching of Silvanus," *Living Buddha, Living Christ* (New York: Riverhead Books, 1997), xxv.

Kushner, Lawrence. *Eyes Remade for Wonder: A Lawrence Kushner Read-er* (Woodstock, VT: Jewish Lights Publishing, 1998), 20–21.

Day 2

Kooser, Ted. *Local Wonders: Seasons in the Bohemian Alps* (Lincoln, NE: Bison Books, 2002).

de Waal, 21.

Day 3

On the CD *We Will Remember*, Carmel Boyle. www.ancroi.ie.

DAY 4

Ladinski, Daniel, trans. *The Gift,* Hafiz (New York: Penguin Books, 1999), 191.

Weems, Ann. "Lament Psalm Six," *Psalms of Lament* (Edinburgh, Scotland: Westminster John Knox Press, 1995), 11.

Weems, "Lament Psalm Twenty-Six," 47.

DAY 5

O'Shaughnessy, Ann, ed. *The Heron Dance Book of Love and Gratitude* (North Ferrisburg, VT: Heron Dance Press, 2005), 35.

DAY 6

Barrows, Anita and Joanna Marie Macy, trans. *Rilke's Book of Hours, Love Poems to God* (New York: Riverhead Publishers, 2005), 52.

WEEK 3

INTRODUCTION

Talarovic, James. trans. *Show Yourself to My Soul: Rabindranath Tagore* (Notre Dame, IN: Sorin Books, 2002), 47.

Douglas-Klotz, Neil. *The Sufi Book of Life: 99 Pathways of the Heart for the Modern Dervish* (New York: Penguin Compass, 2005), 201.

Estés, Clarissa Pinkola. *Women Who Run With the Wolves* (New York: Ballentine Books, 1992), 52.

de Waal, Esther. *A Seven Day Journey with Thomas Merton* (Ann Arbor, MI: Servant Publications, 1992), 68.

Day 1

Wright, Wendy M., ed. *Caryll Houselander: Essential Writings* (Maryknoll, NY: Orbis Books, 2005), 51.

Wood, Nancy. *Dancing Moons* (New York: Doubleday, 1995), 15.

Nouwen, Henri J.M. *Out of Solitude: Three Meditations on Christian Life* (Notre Dame, IN: Ave Maria Press, 1974), 21–22.

Day 2

Markova, 189.

Day 3

Bayrak al-Jerrahi al-Halverti, Sheikh Tosun. *The Most Beautiful Names* (New York: Threshold Books, 1985), 27–28. This may have been listed under a different name.

Day 4

Campbell, Judith. *I Brake for Butterflies, Finding Divinity in All That Is* (Ontario: General Store Publishing House, 2006), 4.

Cannato, Judy. *Radical Amazement* (Notre Dame, IN: Sorin Books, 2006), 138.

Finley, James. Christian Meditation: *Experiencing the Presence of God* (San Francisco: HarperSanFrancisco, 2005), 39.

Day 5

Wiederkehr, 119.

D'Arcy, Paula. *Sacred Threshold: Crossing the Inner Barriers to Deeper Love* (New York: Crossroad Publishing Company, 2004), 111.

Norris, Gunilla. *Inviting Silence: How to Find Inner Silence and Calm* (London: Rider & Co., 2005), 23.

Day 6

Lamott, 121.

I found these words of Carl Jung on a handout from a Jungian seminar. The only source provided for the text is a notation that the message is from Jung's *Collected Works*.

Chödrön, Pema. *Start Where You Are: A Guide to Compassionate Living* (Boston: Shambhala Publications, Inc., 1994), 57–58.

WEEK 4

INTRODUCTION

Arrien, Angeles. *The Second Half of Life* (Louisville, CO: Sounds True, 2005), 9.

Harris, Maria. *Jubilee Time: Celebrating Women, Spirit, and the Advent of Age* (New York: Bantam Books, 1995), 2–3.

Richardson, Jan. L. *Night Visions: Searching the Shadows of Advent and Christmas* (Cleveland, OH: United Church Press, 1998), 110.

DAY 2

Klein, Doris. *Journey of the Soul* (Lanham, MD: Sheed & Ward, 2001), 11.

Kornfield, Jack. "Doing the Buddha's Practice," *Shambhala Sun* (July 2007): 42.

Klein, 12.

DAY 4

Campbell, Joseph. *The Hero with a Thousand Faces* (Princeton, NJ: Princeton University Press, 1972), 92.

Campbell, 69–70.

DAY 5

Nepo, Mark. *The Book of Awakening: Having the Life You Want by Being Present to the Life You Have* (York Beach, ME: Conari Press, 2000), 14.

Finley, 150.

Day 6
Finley, 144.
Finley, 144.
Richardson, 111.

WEEK 5

INTRODUCTION
Douglas-Klotz, 54–55.

Day 1
Palmer, Parker J. *Let Your Life Speak: Listening for the Voice of Vocation* (San Francisco: Jossey-Bass, 2004), 54.

Peers, E. Allison, ed. and trans. *The Interior Castle, Saint Teresa of Avila* (New York: Doubleday, 1961), 29.

Chittister, Joan. *The Story of Ruth: Twelve Moments in Every Woman's Life* (Grand Rapids, MI: William B. Eerdmans Publishing Company, 2000), 20.

Kooser, 83.

Norris, Gunilla. *Being Home: Discovering the Spiritual in the Everyday* (Mahwah, NJ: Hidden Spring, 2001), 69.

Day 2
Harris, 8–9.
Wicks, 80–81.

Day 4
Deignan, Kathleen, ed., and Thomas Merton. *A Book of Hours* (Notre Dame, IN: Sorin Books, 2007), 136.

Peers, 31.

Bruteau, 28.

Douglas-Klotz, 54–55.

Muller, Wayne. *How, Then, Shall We Live? Four Simple Questions That Reveal the Beauty and Meaning of Our Lives* (New York: Bantam Books, 1997), 180.

Day 5

Dass, Ram. *Still Here: Embracing Aging, Changing, and Dying* (New York: Riverhead Books, 2000), 148.

Harvey, Andrew. *The Way of Passion: A Celebration of Rumi* (New York: Tarcher, 2000), 89.

Tobin, Mary Luke. *Hope Is an Open Door* (1981). Printed on a prayer card for her funeral.

Markova, 69.

Talarovic, 145.

Day 6

Ladinski, 222.

Stafford, William. *Even in Quiet Places: Poems* (Lewiston, ID: Confluence Press, 1996), 75.

WEEK 6

Introduction

Barrows and Macy, 84.

Taylor, Barbara Brown. *Leaving Church: A Memoir of Faith* (San Francisco: HarperSanFrancisco, 2006), 165.

Jolley, Gail. *Shift: At the Frontiers of Consciousness*, Letters to the Editor, p. 4.

Day 1

D'Arcy, 45.

O'Donohue, John. *Anam Cara: A Book of Celtic Wisdom* (New York: Bantam Press, 1997), 170.

Pierce, Gregory F.A. *Spirituality at Work: 10 Ways to Balance Your Life on the Job* (Chicago: Loyola Press, 2001), 19.

Orsborn, Carol. *The Art of Resilience: One Hundred Paths to Wisdom and Strength in an Uncertain World.* (New York: Three Rivers Press, 1997), 262.

Day 2

Turley, Jonathan. *USA Today*, Wednesday, April 25, 2007, p. 11A.

Wright, 88–89.

Ellsberg, Robert, ed. *Dorothy Day: Selected Writings* (Maryknoll, NY: Orbis Books, 1983), 224.

Griffin, Emilie, ed. *Evelyn Underhill: Essential Writings* (Maryknoll, NY: Orbis Books, 2003), 58.

Lundy, Brad, and Jan Lundy. *Perfect Love: How to Find Yours and Make It Last Forever* (Traverse City, MI: Heart to Heart Press, 2006), 139.

Day 3

Rucquoi, Adele-Azar. "The Heart's a Loud Voice," *Spirituality and Health* (May-June 2007): 35.

Oliver, Mary. *Long Life: Essays and Other Writings* (Cambridge, MA: De Capo Press, 2004), 13.

Teasdale, Wayne and the Dalai Lama. *The Mystic Heart: Discovering a Universal Spirituality in the World's Religions* (Novato, CA: New World Library, 1999), 123.

Day 4

Nye, Naomi Shihab. "Red Brocade," *19 Varieties of Gazelle: Poems of the Middle East* (New York: HarperTempest, 1994), 40.

Day 5

King, Martin Luther, Jr. "The World House," *Shift: At the Frontier of Consciousness* (Dec. 2006–Feb. 2007): 35.

Day 6

Vandana Shiva, quoted in Korten, David C. *The Great Turning: From Empire to Earth Community* (Bloomfield, CT: Kumarian Press, Inc., 2006), 357.

APPENDIX

WEEK 3: PROCESS AND PRAYER

Talarovic, 37.
Talarovic, 36.

WEEK 4: PROCESS AND PRAYER

Richardson, 115.

WEEK 6: PROCESS AND PRAYER

Whyte, David. "The Winter of Listening," *River Flow: New and Selected Poems* (Langly, WA: Many Rivers Press, 2007), 19.
Novotka, Jan. "All I Do Today," in *The Name of All That Is.* The word "today" in the song is changed to "each day" in this prayer form.
Roberts, Elizabeth, and Elias Amidon, eds. "The Shiddur of Shir Chadash," *Life Prayers from Around the World* (San Francisco: HarperSanFrancisco, 1996), 261. I have adapted the prayer for this week's gathering.

BIBLIOGRAPHY

Alvarez, Julia. *The Woman I Kept to Myself.* Chapel Hill, NC: Algonquin Books of Chapel Hill, 2004.

Arrien, Angeles. *The Second Half of Life.* Louisville, CO: Sounds True, 2005.

Atwood, Margaret. *The Door: Poems.* New York: Houghton Mifflin Co., 2007.

Barasch, Marc Ian. *Field Notes on the Compassionate Life.* New York: Rodale, 2005.

Barks, Coleman, trans. *The Essential Rumi.* Edison, NJ: Castle Books, 1995.

Barrows, Anita, and Joanna Macy, trans. *Rilke's Book of Hours, Love Poems to God.* New York: Riverhead Books, 1996.

Bayrak al-Jerrahi al-Halverti, Sheikh Tosun. *The Most Beautiful Names.* New York: Threshold Books, 1985.

Bolen, Jean Shinoda, MD. *Urgent Message from Mother: Gather the Women, Save the World.* York Beach, ME: Conari Press, 2005.

Bruteau, Beatrice. *Easter Mysteries.* New York: Crossroad Publishing Company, 1995.

———. *What We Can Learn From the East*. New York: Crossroad Publishing Company, 1995.

Burnett, Frances Hodgson. *The Secret Garden*. New York: Bantam Books, 1987.

Campbell, Joseph. *The Hero with a Thousand Faces*. Princeton, NJ: Princeton University Press, 1972.

Campbell, Judith. *I Brake for Butterflies, Finding Divinity in All That Is*. Ontario: General Store Publishing House, 2006.

Cannato, Judy. *Radical Amazement*. Notre Dame, IN: Sorin Books, 2006.

Chittister, Joan. *The Story of Ruth: Twelve Moments in Every Woman's Life*. Grand Rapids, MI: William B. Eerdmans Publishing Company, 2000.

Chödrön, Pema. *Start Where You Are: A Guide to Compassionate Living*. Boston: Shambhala Publications, Inc., 1994.

Cowley, Joy. *Psalms for the Road*. Central Hawkes Bay, New Zealand: Pleroma Press, 2002.

D'Arcy, Paula. *Sacred Threshold: Crossing the Inner Barriers to Deeper Love*. New York: Crossroad Publishing Company, 2004.

Dass, Ram. *Still Here: Embracing Aging, Changing, and Dying*. New York: Riverhead Books, 2000.

Deignan, Kathleen, ed., and Thomas Merton. *A Book of Hours*. Notre Dame, IN: Sorin Books, 2007.

de Waal, Esther. *Lost in Wonder: Rediscovering the Spiritual Art of Attentiveness*. Norwich, Norfolk: Canterbury Press, 2003.

———. *A Seven Day Journey with Thomas Merton*. Ann Arbor, MI: Servant Publications, 1992.

Douglas-Klotz, Neil. *The Sufi Book of Life: 99 Pathways of the Heart for the Modern Dervish*. New York: Penguin Compass, 2005.

Ellsberg, Robert, ed. *Dorothy Day: Selected Writings*. Maryknoll, NY: Orbis Books, 1983.

Estés, Clarissa Pinkola. *Women Who Run with the Wolves*. New York: Ballentine Books, 1992.

Finley, James. *Christian Meditation: Experiencing the Presence of God*. San Francisco: HarperSanFrancisco, 2005.

_____. *Merton's Palace of Nowhere*. Notre Dame, IN: Ave Maria Press, 1978, 2003.

Griffin, Emilie, ed. *Evelyn Underhill: Essential Writings*. Maryknoll, NY: Orbis Books, 2003.

Hanh, Thich Nhat. *Living Buddha, Living Christ*. New York: Riverhead Books, 1995.

Harris, Maria. *Jubilee Time: Celebrating Women, Spirit, and the Advent of Age*. New York: Bantam Books, 1995.

Harvey, Andrew. *The Way of Passion: A Celebration of Rumi*. New York: Tarcher, 2000.

Harvey, Andrew, and Eryk Hanut. *Perfume of the Desert: Inspirations from Sufi Wisdom*. Wheaton, IL: Quest Books, 1999.

Ironside, Elizabeth. *Death in the Garden*. New York: Felony & Mayhem, 2005.

Kidd, Sue Monk. *The Secret Life of Bees*. New York: Penguin Publishing, 2003.

King, Ursula, ed. *Pierre Teilhard de Chardin: Selected Writings*. Maryknoll, NY: Orbis Books, 1999.

Klein, Doris. *Journey of the Soul*. Lanham, MD: Sheed & Ward, 2001.

Kooser, Ted. *Local Wonders: Seasons in the Bohemian Alps*. Lincoln, NE: Bison Books, 2002.

Kornfield, Jack. *A Path with Heart*. New York: Bantam Books, 1993.

Korten, David C. *The Great Turning: From Empire to Earth Community*. Bloomfield, CT: Kumarian Press, Inc., 2006.

Ladinsky, Daniel. *The Gift, Poems by Hafiz*. New York: Penguin, 1999.

Lamott, Anne. *Grace (Eventually): Thoughts on Faith*. New York: Riverhead Books, 2007.

Leder, Drew. *Sparks of the Divine*. Notre Dame, IN: Sorin Books, 2004.

Lundy, Brad, and Jan Lundy. *Perfect Love: How to Find Yours and Make It Last Forever*. Traverse City, MI: Heart to Heart Press, 2006.

Markova, Dawna. *I Will Not Die an Unlived Life: Reclaiming Purpose and Passion*. York Beach, ME: Conari Press, 2000.

McKenna, Megan. *And Morning Came: Scriptures of the Resurrection*. Lanham, MD: Sheed & Ward, 2002.

Muller, Wayne. *How, Then, Shall We Live? Four Simple Questions That Reveal the Beauty and Meaning of Our Lives*. New York: Bantam Books, 1997.

Nepo, Mark. *The Book of Awakening: Having the Life You Want by Being Present to the Life You Have*. York Beach, ME: Conari Press, 2000.

Norris, Gunilla. *Being Home: Discovering the Spiritual in the Everyday*. Mahwah, NJ: Hidden Spring, 2001.

Nouwen, Henri J.M. *Out of Solitude: Three Meditations on Christian Life*. Notre Dame, IN: Ave Maria Press, 1974.

Nye, Naomi Shihab. *19 Varieties of Gazelle: Poems of the Middle East*. New York: HarperTempest, 1994.

O'Donohue, John. *Anam Cara: A Book of Celtic Wisdom*. New York: Bantam Press, 1997.

Oliver, Mary. *Long Life: Essays and Other Writings*. Cambridge, MA: De Capo Press, 2004.

Orsborn, Carol. *The Art of Resilience: One Hundred Paths to Wisdom and Strength in an Uncertain World*. New York: Three Rivers Press, 1997.

Palmer, Parker J. *Let Your Life Speak: Listening for the Voice of Vocation*. San Francisco: Jossey-Bass, 2004.

Peers, E. Allison, ed. and trans. *The Interior Castle, Saint Teresa of Avila*. New York: Doubleday, 1961.

Pierce, Gregory F.A. *Spirituality at Work: 10 Ways to Balance Your Life on the Job*. Chicago: Loyola Press, 2001.

Prétat, Jane R. *Coming to Age: The Croning Years and Late-Life Transformation*. Toronto: Inner City Books, 1994.

Richardson, Jan L. *Night Visions: Searching the Shadows of Advent and Christmas*. Cleveland, OH: United Church Press, 1998.

Rowling, J.K. *Harry Potter and the Sorcerer's Stone*. New York: A.A. Levine Books, 1998.

Senge, Peter, Otto C. Scharmer, Joseph Jaworski, and Betty Sue Flowers. *Presence*. New York: Doubleday, 2005.

Stafford, William. *Even in Quiet Places: Poems*. Lewiston, ID: Confluence Press, 1996.

Suzuki, Shunryu. *Zen Mind, Beginner's Mind*. Boston: Weatherhill, Inc., 1970.

Tagore, Rabindranath. *Gitanjali*. New York: MacMillan Publishing, 1971.

Talarovic, James, trans. *Show Yourself to My Soul: Rabindranath Tagore*. Notre Dame, IN: Sorin Books, 2002.

Taylor, Barbara Brown. *Leaving Church: A Memoir of Faith*. San Francisco: HarperSanFrancisco, 2006.

Teasdale, Wayne, and the Dalai Lama. *The Mystic Heart: Discovering a Universal Spirituality in the World's Religions*. Novato, CA: New World Library, 1999.

Walters, Dorothy. *Marrow of Flame: Poems of the Spiritual Journey*. Prescott, AZ: Hohm Press, 2000.

Weems, Ann. *Psalms of Lament*. Edinburgh, Scotland: Westminster John Knox Press, 1995.

Whyte, David. *River Flow: New and Selected Poems*. Langly, WA: Many Rivers Press, 2007.

Wicks, Robert J. *Crossing the Desert: Learning to Let Go, Live Simply, and See Clearly*. Notre Dame, IN: Sorin Books, 2007.

Wiederkehr, Macrina. *The Song of the Seed: The Monastic Way of Tending the Soul.* San Francisco: HarperSanFrancisco, 1995.

Winterson, Jeanette. *Lighthousekeeping.* New York: Harcourt, Inc., 2004.

Wood, Nancy. *Dancing Moons.* New York: Doubleday, 1995.

Wright, Wendy M., ed. *Caryll Houselander: Essential Writings.* Maryknoll, NY: Orbis Books, 2005.

Acknowledgments *(continued from p. iv)*

Lyrics from "My Soul's Desire" are used with permission of Carmel Boyle, www.ancroi.ie. All rights reserved.

Excerpt from *Psalms of Lament* by Ann Weems, © 1995 Ann Weems, used with permission of Westminster John Knox Press.

Excerpt from *Marrow of Flame: Poems of the Spiritual Journey* by Dorothy Walters, copyright © 2000 by Dorothy Walters, is used with permission of Hohm Press, Prescott, AZ.

"Du, Nachbar, Gott . . . / You God who live next door . . . *Du wist nur mir der Tat erfast*," from *Rilke's Book of Hours, Love Poems to God* translated by Anita Barrows and Joanna Marie Macy, © 1996 by Anita Barrows and Joanna Macy is used with permission of Riverhead Books, a division of Penguin Group (USA) Inc.

Excerpt from "The Door" from *The Door* by Margaret Atwood. Copyright © 2007 by O.W. Toad Ltd. is reprinted with permission of Houghton Mifflin Harcourt Co. All rights reserved.

Excerpt from *Inviting Silence* by Gunilla Norris, Copyright © 2004 by Gunilla Norris, is used with permission of BlueBridge Publishing.

Excerpts from *Being Home: Discovering the Spiritual in the Everyday* by Gunilla Norris, copyright © 1991 by Gunilla Norris, are reprinted with permission of Paulist Press, Inc. www.paulistpress.com.

Excerpt from "It Returns at Times " in *Even in Quiet Places* by William Stafford, copyright © 1996 William Stafford, is reprinted with permission of Confluence Press.

Excerpt from *The Art of Resilience* by Carol Orsborn, copyright © 1997 by Carol Orsborn, is used with permission of Three Rivers Press, a division of Random House Inc.

Excerpts from *Night Visions* by Jan L Richardson, copyright © 1998 by Jan L Richardson, is used with permission of the author. All rights reserved.

"The Winter of Listening" by David Whyte from *River Flow: New and Selected Poems*, copyright © 2007 David Whyte, is reprinted with permission of Many Rivers Press, Langley, WA. www.davidwhyte.com.

Lyrics of "All I Do Today" and "The Presence You Are" by Jan Novotka, copyright © 2006 by Jan Novotka's Music LLC, are used with permission. All rights reserved.

Excerpt from by *The Woman I Kept to Myself*, copyright © 2004 by Julia Alvarez, published by Algonquin Books of Chapel Hill in 2004, reprinted with permission of Susan Bergholz Literary Services, New York, NY, and Lamy, NM. All rights reserved.

JOYCE RUPP is well known for her work as a writer, spiritual "midwife," and retreat and conference speaker. A member of the Servite (Servants of Mary) community, she has led retreats throughout North America, as well as in Europe, Asia, Africa, Australia and New Zealand. Joyce is the author of many books, including bestsellers *Rest Your Dreams on a Little Twig*, *The Cup of Our Life*, *May I Have This Dance?*, and *Praying Our Goodbyes*. Visit her website at www.joycerupp.com.

More from Joyce Rupp

May I Have This Dance?
An Invitation to Faithful Prayer Throughout the Year
This revised edition of Joyce Rupp's best-selling book invites readers to join God in the dance of life, a dance of truth and wholeness. She explores twelve themes, each followed by prayer suggestions such as litanies, guided meditations, and journal keeping. *A gifted and trusted spiritual guide with a sure hand, she exposes the fear of change that keeps us resistant to the dance.* —**Paula D'Arcy**, Author of *Gift of the Red Bird*
ISBN: 9781594711329 / 224 pages / $14.95

May I Have This Dance?
Guided Meditations
Experience a peace-filled being and an attuned connection with your spirit as you accept Rupp's invitation to dance with the Divine Partner through twelve guided mediations. For use alone or as a companion to Rupp's newly revised *May I Have This Dance?*
ISBN: 9781594711671 / 2 CDs, 137 min./ $16.95

The Circle of Life
The Heart's Journey Through the Seasons
Joyce Rupp and Macrina Wiederkehr
Artwork by Mary Southard
Reflections, poems, prayers, and meditations help us to explore the relationship between the seasons of the earth and the seasons of our lives. *A reflective resource for individuals and groups whose goal is to deepen the inner life.* —**Presence**
ISBN: 9781893732827 / 288 pages / $19.95

Fresh Bread
And Other Gifts of Spiritual Nourishment
This popular classic introduced a hungry world to Joyce Rupp's unique brand of spiritual nourishment: prose, poetry, and prayer to help us reflect upon and rejoice in the sacred world around and within us. This twentieth-anniversary edition reveals insights about the budding of Rupp's own spirituality and illustrates the ongoing relevance of *Fresh Bread* in today's world.
Solidly grounded in scripture, it is a yeasty resource for all hungry for a deeper prayer life. —**Heidi Schlumpf**, Managing Editor, *U.S. Catholic*
ISBN: 9781594710858 / 160 pages / $12.95

The Cup of Our Life
A Guide for Spiritual Growth
Explores how the cup is a symbol of life, with its emptiness and fullness, its brokenness and flaws, and all of its blessings.
ISBN: 9780877936251 / 184 pages / $15.95

ave maria press®

Available from your bookstore or from
ave maria press / Notre Dame, IN 46556
www.avemariapress.com / Ph: 800-282-1865
A Ministry of the Indiana Province of Holy Cross

Keycode: FD9Ø6Ø8ØØØØ